MARY

What the Bible Really Says

DOUGLAS CONNELLY

InterVarsity Press
Downers Grove, Illinois

InterVarsity Press
P.O. Box 1400, Downers Grove, IL 60515
World Wide Web: www.ivpress.com
E-mail: mail@ivpress.com

*InterVarsity Press® is the book-publishing division of InterVarsity Christian Fellowship/USA®, a
student movement active on campus at hundreds of universities, colleges and schools of nursing in the
United States of America, and a member movement of the International Fellowship of Evangelical
Students. For information about local and regional activities, write Public Relations Dept.,
InterVarsity Christian Fellowship/USA, 6400 Schroeder Rd., P.O. Box 7895, Madison, WI
53707-7895.*

All Scripture quotations, unless otherwise indicated, are taken from the Holy Bible, New
International Version®. NIV®. *Copyright ©1973, 1978, 1984 by International Bible Society. Used
by permission of Zondervan Publishing House. All rights reserved.*

Map illustration by Rich Tesner, Renset Graphic Design, Flushing, Michigan.

Cover illustration: Madonna and Child by Giovanni Bellini/Superstock

ISBN 0-8308-1950-9

Printed in the United States of America ♾

Library of Congress Cataloging-in-Publication Data

Connelly, Douglas, 1949-
   Mary : what the Bible really says / Douglas Connelly.
     p. cm.
   Includes bibliographical references.
   ISBN 0-8308-1950-9
   1. Mary, Blessed Virgin, Saint—Biblical teaching. 2. Bible.
N.T.—Criticism, interpretation, etc. I. Title.
 BT611.C65 1998
 232.91—dc21   *97-49088*
                                                                   CIP

20	19	18	17	16	15	14	13	12	11	10	9	8	7	6	5	4	3	2	1
14	13	12	11	10	09	08	07	06	05	04	03	02	01	00	99	98			

To Karen

Acknowledgments

I want to thank several people who have helped me, prayed for me and encouraged me as I've worked on this book. Tom Skaff and Steve Aikman use our accountability meetings to keep me on track and to remind me of my deadlines. Ken Gilbert, Dick Adomat, Matt Johnson, Rich Tesner, Charles Layzell and Bill Sobey are faithful to pray for me. I also have some friends in pastoral ministry who provide a sounding board for my ideas and my heresies—David Thompson in Pocatello, Idaho; Neal Rylaarsdam in Portage, Michigan; Bill Lepley in Grabill, Indiana; and Phil Burch around the corner. They are great guys.

Cindy Bunch-Hotaling and all the people at InterVarsity Press do a superb job in shepherding my books to print and to bookstores. They are the best.

This book is dedicated to my wife, Karen. She is a wonderful model in my life of the character of Mary and of Mary's son. She has held me, and held on to me, through some difficult storms. She has the unique ability to build me up when I need it and bring me back to reality when I need it. Karen, my children, my parents and my gracious church family at Cross make my life full and rich.

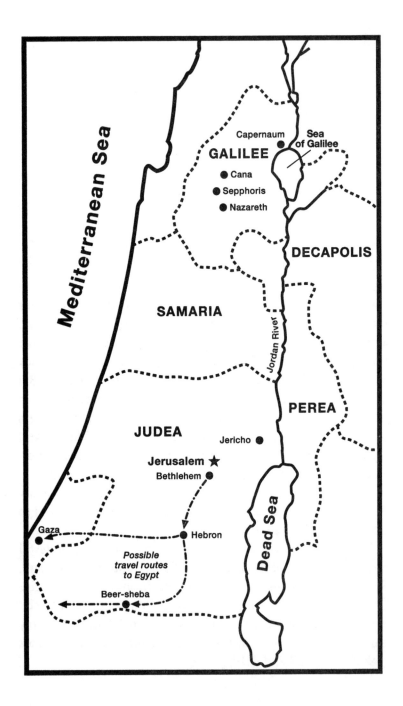

Chapter 1

MEETING MARY FOR THE FIRST TIME

*M*ary *makes us nervous. Some Christians have exalted Mary* so high that we feel like we can never attain her level of virtue. She is (as I heard one university student call her) "the saint of all saints." She stands in dramatic contrast to the failure and struggle we experience every day. We stutter in the presence of such perfection.

Other Christians have ignored Mary. They aren't interested in looking seriously at her life or character. For many of us Mary is little more than a figurine in the nativity set that we dust off each year and put away.

Who is this woman? Is she a saint of such perfect character that we can't even begin to identify with her? Was she above all of the personal problems and insecurities that we wrestle with? How can we simply ignore her when the Bible tells us so much about her godliness and courageous obedience to God? One part of the Christian community lifts Mary almost to the level of deity while another part finds it easier to confine her to Christmas pageants and sentimental Christmas cards. I'm afraid that if most of us were asked to name the great women of faith in the Bible we would quickly picture Ruth gleaning in the fields of Boaz or Mary of Bethany anointing Jesus with precious oil, but we would not even think of Jesus' mother.

My own interest in Mary began as I faced another series of Christmas messages. There just aren't that many ways to tell the same story every year! I had preached on the stable and the shepherds so many times that I could see my congregation lulled to sleep by the familiar scenes and the traditional platitudes. As I thought about how to approach the series, I realized that the Christmas story was wrapped around people—men and women we think we know but who have never taken on much life of their own. I began to ask questions of everyone connected to the birth of Jesus. How did Joseph feel when he discovered that Mary was pregnant? What was the stable really like, and what about that lout of an innkeeper who turned Mary and Joseph away? We've always pictured him as an unshaven, grumpy old guy with a can of Budweiser in his hand, turning our poor heroes out into the cold. But was he being cruel? And was it cold on that night two thousand years ago?

The questions forced me back to the Bible and into the culture of first-century Palestine. I tried to lay aside everything I had simply believed about the birth of Jesus and I began to look at the story with fresh eyes and a seeking heart. Not only did my study make for some interesting Christmas preaching (at least no one fell asleep!), it also stirred a deep interest in Mary as a model of submission and obedience to God. For years I had just skimmed over the passages that unfold Mary's character. Several times I had pointed to men in the Scriptures as examples of godliness, but here was a woman who challenged my commitment to Christ at every turn!

When I looked at Mary as a parent, she exposed my stunning lack of sacrifice and devotion to my own children. When I looked at Mary as a believer, she marked out a path of obedience to God that I have rarely had the courage to follow. I discovered to my embarrassment that for all the years of my Christian experience I had neglected a powerful role model. Mary is far more than a cold mosaic on a church wall. She draws us into a life of humble vulnerability and courageous loyalty to the Lord God.

My purpose in writing this book is to take you with me as I walk the path of Mary's life. I will focus on the New Testament and what we can learn about Mary from the record of God's Word. Some of the details we can fill in from our knowledge of Jewish culture in the first century. Questions about other details of Mary's life have to be left unanswered. My goal is to rescue Mary from the centuries of tradition and legend that have wrapped themselves around her. I feel like an art restorationist working on a magnificent portrait. The original beauty and power of the painting can be seen only when the old varnish and dirt have been meticulously removed. I will try to show you the true picture of Mary—a portrait drawn from Scripture with much of the overlay of tradition and the dust of neglect removed.

I realize that I will be treading on some very controversial ground. As I've talked to friends about this book, they almost immediately raised some tough questions. What about the people who see visions of Mary or claim to receive messages from her? What about the teaching of the Catholic Church or Orthodox churches about Mary? Where does that come from?

I am writing from the perspective of evangelical Protestant belief. We will look at several of the beliefs of the Catholic and Orthodox churches, but my goal is not simply to criticize the teaching of others. I have tried to present their views accurately. I've also tried to examine their beliefs about Mary from a biblical perspective. I will also try to help you evaluate the claims of those who say they have seen visions of Mary, but I am convinced that once you see Mary as she is presented in God's Word, these claimed visions will dim to insignificance.

My primary focus throughout the book is on the rediscovery of the Mary of the Bible. The clear light of Scripture will equip us to evaluate the traditions that have grown up around Mary and that have at times almost blocked her from view.

I hope you are ready to look at Mary with fresh eyes and a seeking heart. What you see might just transform your walk with the Lord beyond all recognition. You will never again be able to look at the figurine in the nativity set in the same way. God is still seeking men and women like Mary who will fearlessly respond to his call.

An Awakening Heart

When Mary was born, the golden age of Israel's proud history was past. No king of David's family had ruled in Jerusalem for well over five hundred years. Centuries of time and decades of upheaval had allowed the branches of the royal family tree to scatter into oblivion. The people of Israel, however, had not forgotten God's promise that a deliverer would come from David's seed. As proud as the Jews were of their glorious past, they were looking for an even more glorious future. Every believing heart in Israel longed for the Messiah.

Very little is known for certain about Mary's early life. The hints we have from the New Testament and the inferences we can draw from our knowledge of the culture into which she was born point to a humble, godly upbringing. Mary's father, apparently, was a descendant of the great king David through David's son Nathan. Undoubtedly her father was very proud of his family's lineage and tried to bear the weight of his heritage with dignity.

Mary's mother had ties directly or indirectly to the clan of Levi, the priests of Israel. Mary's relative, Elizabeth, was of the tribe of Levi and the family of Aaron, the first high priest of Israel. The spiritual devotion in Mary's childhood home would have been intensified by the priestly influence from her mother's family. The Sabbath and feast days were observed with joyful obedience. God's Word in the Law and the Psalms was read and sung and discussed around the table or in the quiet evenings. Mary's character was formed and refined by what she saw modeled in her home.

The Protoevangelium of James, a book written long after the New Testament was completed, claims to tell the story of Mary's birth and early life. The document is an apocryphal gospel; it was never considered accurate or authoritative by early Christians. Most apocryphal books of the second or third century were more romance novel than historical record. From this source we are told that Mary's parents were Joachim and Anne.

Another tradition centered on Mary's family is that Mary was an only child. The apostle John, however, says that as Mary stood near Jesus' cross, her sister stood with her (John 19:25). Because Mary is in Galilee when she first appears in the biblical story, most interpreters of Scripture believe that Mary was born in Nazareth. But there are other fairly reliable traditions that Mary was born in Bethlehem, in Sepphoris (a city near Nazareth) or even in Jerusalem. Mary came to Nazareth (so the tradition tells us) when her parents died early in her life.

I am convinced that Mary's first impressions as a child were centered on devotion to God and to God's Word. Her own knowledge of Scripture and her later godly character point to early years of biblical instruction and faithful observance of God's Law. "Hear, O Israel, the Lord our God is one Lord" were the opening words of the Shema, the Jewish affirmation of faith recited by the father of the household twice every day. The prayers of adoration and the stories of the Bible were spoken with enthusiasm and were heard with eagerness. These were the life stories of Mary's own people. Most of the biblical events took place within a hundred miles of her front door.

The proper education of children was considered a solemn responsibility of the entire community. Synagogue schools were free, supported by the contributions of the local congregation. Boys and girls were taught (in separate classrooms) to read and probably to write. The Jews were people of the Book, and every member of the covenant community needed to be able to read the precepts and promises in the Scriptures.

A large part of Mary's education was conducted at home. Women married at a young age, and they had to be equipped to manage a household. Mary learned to prepare meals and to weave fabric for clothes. The sophisticated citizens of Jerusalem had their pick of fine linen and wool and even finished garments from India or Egypt, but in the rural areas of Galilee most fabrics were still made by hand and lovingly fashioned into a family's wardrobe. There was nothing glamorous or romantic about a woman's life in Palestine in the first century. She worked long hours just to maintain her household.

Long weeks of work were broken only by the rest of the sabbath day and by the cycle of festivals designed to remind the Jews of God's great power and daily provision. The feast of Passover in the spring, the celebration of Pentecost in the summer and the festival of Tabernacles in the fall provided time for focused worship and social pleasure. Probably Mary's older relative Elizabeth visited often enough for a warm bond of love and trust to develop between the two women. Later, in a time of crisis, Elizabeth was the woman Mary turned to for strength and encouragement.

Making It Personal

Long, relatively uneventful years of teaching and parenting laid the foundation of Mary's character. We don't know who God may be preparing in our homes or in the Sunday-school class we teach. We may spend our lives in relative obscurity, but we may also be the instruments God uses to develop a man or woman who will mark a generation—or the rest of human history—for good and for God. Mary's parents and teachers and role models are virtually unknown, but their combined influence produced a woman of remarkable strength.

As Mary reached her early teens, her parents began to plan for her marriage to a suitable young man. Most marriage agreements were made when the children were very young. Mary's parents chose wisely. Their daughter was promised to a man training to be a carpenter. Joseph was a gentle, hardworking man, fully committed to the Lord. When he completed training in his trade, the announcement was made in the synagogue that Joseph and Mary were officially engaged. Family and friends showered congratulations on the young couple, and preparations began for the wedding one year later. Within a few months, however, circumstances would dramatically change for the couple. God would break in on their lives with astonishing news—news that would alter their lives forever.

Chapter 2

LISTENING
TO AN ANGEL

*W*hen *Mary first appears in the pages of Scripture, she is in* the presence of a magnificent angel. Four times in Scripture the angel Gabriel leaves the heavenly presence of God to come to men and women uniquely chosen and blessed by God—and he always brings a message of hope! He came twice to the prophet Daniel to assure him in the dark days of Israel's captivity that the Lord God had not forgotten his people or his promises to bless them (Daniel 8:15-16; 9:21). Five hundred years later Gabriel appeared to an old priest as he served in the temple (Luke 1:19). The angel told Zechariah that God had not forgotten his people. God's plan was right on schedule. Zechariah and his wife, Elizabeth, would have a son who would prepare the way for the Messiah, the Lord himself.

Now six months after the announcement to Zechariah, Gabriel is sent by God again to a little town in Palestine. He comes to announce to a teenage girl that she has been chosen by God to bear in her body the holy Son of God. God is coming to earth.

I'm impressed that God did not send Gabriel to the emperor's court in Rome or to a member of one of the leading Jewish families in Jerusalem. God's blessing came to a backwater village on the fringe of the Roman Empire. First-century Nazareth was famous for only one thing—its sin. It was located just four miles from the Roman garrison at Sepphoris. When the boys in the army got a few days leave and some bonus pay, they went to Nazareth, where they could find cheap wine and cheaper women. It was probably Nazareth's "red-light" reputation that led a critic of Christianity two and a half centuries after Jesus' birth to accuse Mary of having a child "by a certain soldier named Panthera."[1]

In Nazareth Gabriel speaks to a young woman. Mary is probably only thirteen or fourteen years old, the customary age for betrothal and marriage in rural Jewish areas. I remember looking at my own daughter not that many years ago and being shocked to realize how young Mary was when the angel's brilliance surrounded her. Gabriel's first words are startling: "Greetings, you who are highly favored! The Lord is with you" (Luke 1:28). The word translated "favored" means to receive grace.[2] Later Gabriel will add, "Mary, you have found favor with God" (v. 30), or "you have become the recipient of God's grace."

We have been under the impression that Mary was chosen by God to bear his Son because of something righteous in Mary. Gabriel makes it clear, however, that Mary was chosen by God as an act of grace. Mary's blessedness derived from God's grace, not from some inherent goodness of her own. Mary will confirm with her own testimony that she, like every other human being, needed a Savior.

Even Mary's response to the angel's greeting demonstrates her humility and sense of unease. Luke writes, "Mary was greatly troubled"—not at the angel's *presence* but at the angel's *words* (v. 29). When the angel says, "You, Mary, are greatly favored with the grace of God," her response in essence is "Why me? I have nothing good in myself to offer God. Why would he choose me?"

Gabriel senses Mary's surprise and concern and reassures her, "Do not be afraid, Mary." Then he makes an incredible announcement: "You will be with child and give birth to a son, and you are to give him the name Jesus. He will be great and will be called the Son of the Most High. The Lord God will give him the throne of his father David, and he will reign over the house of Jacob forever; his kingdom will never end" (Luke 1:31-33). The emphasis of Gabriel's message was on the child, not on Mary. Mary was the vessel chosen by God to bear his Son, and therefore she was greatly blessed. But far overshadowing Mary was the character of the child she would bear. This child would be all that the Old Testament prophets said he would be. He would reign as the greatest king Israel had ever seen, a greater and mightier man than even King David. David reigned for forty years and then died. In the last years of his reign one son after another rose in rebellion to claim the kingdom as his own. But Mary's child will reign forever. His kingdom will never languish under the limitations of earthly kingdoms.

But this promised son would be much more than a great man; he would be called the Son of the Most High. In the Jewish mind, to say that a person was "the son" of someone meant that the person shared the same inherent nature as the one called father. When Jesus told some hardhearted critics that they were "of their father, the devil," he was pointing out that they possessed a fallen, rebellious nature exactly like Satan's

(John 8:44). When Gabriel said that Jesus would be "the Son of the Most High," it meant that Mary's child would have the nature of God himself. This son would be deity—God in human flesh.

Because Mary's son would be God among us, he could be the one who finally would release humanity from sin's stranglehold. The boy's name was to be Jesus, a contraction of the Hebrew name Yehoshua (or Joshua), which meant "the Lord saves." The name summarized the whole purpose of the child's birth. God was coming to earth to rescue his people.

Mary had no trouble understanding *who* this child would be. He would be the promised Messiah, God's unique Son, Immanuel—God with us. Mary's only question was *how* it would be accomplished. "How will this be . . . since I am a virgin?" (Luke 1:34). Mary's question was not one of doubt or unbelief. She believed what the angel said. She just wanted to know how the promise would be fulfilled. Mary's testimony before an angel of God was that she had never been sexually intimate with Joseph or with any other man. The only way Mary could imagine that she could bear a child was through a sexual encounter with a man. But Gabriel's answer to her question opened a whole new possibility. "The angel answered, 'The Holy Spirit will come upon you, and the power of the Most High will overshadow you. So the holy one to be born will be called the Son of God' " (v. 35).

How is it that Mary as a virgin conceived a child? How did the eternal God become a human being? The Bible's answer is that it was a miraculous work of God—God did it! Jesus was conceived in Mary by the power of the Holy Spirit.

As confirmation of his message, Gabriel tells Mary about Elizabeth, Mary's relative,[3] a woman more than sixty years old who had been unable to bear children but who now is in the sixth month of her pregnancy. As unbelievable as it seemed,

Elizabeth had conceived in her old age, and Mary would conceive too. But the conception in Mary would be far more miraculous than the one in Elizabeth. Mary would conceive a child by the power of the Holy Spirit.

Then Gabriel adds a stunning promise: "For nothing is impossible with God." A literal translation of that sentence reads, "For no word from God will be empty of power." Gabriel was assuring Mary that God will do everything he promises to do. Gabriel's theme is the same as it was when he spoke to Daniel and to Zechariah: God keeps his promises.

Can you imagine what thoughts must have gone through Mary's mind as she listened to Gabriel's announcement about the child she would conceive? We normally rush from the angel's declaration directly to Mary's acceptance, and we think that her submission to the will of God came easily. But we know from other passages of Scripture that Mary was a very reflective person. Even in this passage, Mary "wondered" over the angel's greeting (v. 29). She was the kind of person who observed carefully. She took in all the facts and then thought deeply about the significance of those facts in her life. As Mary listened to the angel she must have wrestled with the consequences that would come in her life if she accepted God's call.

I teach a class for Spring Arbor College called Biblical Perspectives. The students are in an off-campus degree completion program, and most of them have had very little exposure to the Bible. We were discussing Mary's encounter with the angel Gabriel one evening, and I asked the class what concerns must have lingered in Mary's mind as she heard Gabriel's words. One student said, "How could she have any doubts or questions? She was hearing this from *an angel!*" Unfortunately that's how most of us respond to the story. We read Mary's words in verse 38 and think they came easily: " 'I am the Lord's servant,' Mary answered. 'May it be to me as you have said.' " But as the class thought more deeply about the cost of Mary's submission to God, several observations emerged. Mary's willing acceptance of the will of God began with a song in her heart, but it ended with a sword in her own soul. The joy of holding a beautiful baby led ultimately to the foot of a cross.

One young woman in the class very perceptively noted that the angel came only to Mary. His announcement wasn't written in the sky over Nazareth for all the people to read. The student's comment was "Imagine trying to explain *this* to your family!" Mary would live her whole life under a cloud of suspicion from her family and neighbors. Even Jesus was accused of being conceived immorally. When Jesus exposed the evil intentions of some of his accusers, they shot back at him, "*We* are not illegitimate children" (John 8:41).

Mary had no guarantee that her beloved Joseph would understand or even believe her story of a miraculous conception. Mary had to face the man she loved and tell him that she was pregnant—and Joseph knew *he* wasn't the father. Embedded in Mary's decision to be fully submissive to the call of God was her willingness to suffer ridicule and contempt and loneliness. God certainly didn't force this choice on Mary; she willingly embraced what God had for her. But the decision was made with no assurance that anyone except God would ever fully understand.

Making It Personal
Mary was willing to pay a high price in order to submit to the call of God. All the rest of the events in her life, her place in Scripture and her place in God's plan can be traced back to this one momentous decision to be the servant, the bondslave, of the Lord. It's at this point that Mary speaks so powerfully to us. Obedience to God *always* costs.

The young woman or young man who determines to live a life of purity before the Lord may pay the price of popularity on campus. Obedience to God's Word may cost you your boyfriend or girlfriend or best friend, and you may never be able to explain. The businessperson who decides to live according to biblical priorities instead of the world's priorities may pay the price in lost promotions or a lower salary. The missionary who labors in a faraway culture may pay a heavy price in loneliness and lack of prestige or affirmation, and in addition may have very few tangible "results" to point to at the end of years of struggle. Mary put her reputation on the line in order to obey God.

Opportunities for radical obedience to God can come to us at any time in our lives and in an infinite variety of circumstances. Chris Hall is a optometrist who runs a eye clinic in one of the roughest neighborhoods in our city. He does it not because it earns him money but because the people in that area need the service that he provides. Does he gain great acclaim for his sacrifice? Very few people even know about his work. Could he earn more money operating his more suburban clinic full time? Of course. But he quietly offers up his work as an act of sacrifice to the Lord.

My parents, Paul and Mary Connelly, spent the first full year of their retirement in a mission hospital in the Ivory Coast. They could have stayed close to home and family and saved the money they spent on their mission work, but the Lord put a burden on their hearts and they responded. Dick Adomat spends several hours a week at our local county jail working as a chaplain to prisoners. Dick could find plenty of things—good things—to do with those hours, but as he listened one Sunday morning to a challenge about prison ministry, God put a call on his life. And Dick responded obediently. Ron and Leslie Radke and their young son, Nathan, left the comfort and security of their home and family to go to the Aka Pygmies in the African nation of Congo. Years of theological and linguistic training, hard months of support raising and the incredible loneliness of life in an isolated village setting have been invested in hopes of bringing the Scriptures to the Aka in their own language.

Whatever God's call to obedience costs in your life and my life, Mary stands as proof that submission to God is worth it. For two thousand years believing men and women have seen in Mary a woman who trusted God and who as a result was greatly blessed by God's grace. Mary had the privilege that no other woman in human history had. She was the chosen vessel through whom God the Son became human. Her exaltation, however, only came after her willing heart said, "I am the Lord's servant. Whatever it costs, wherever it takes me, I will do it."

Chapter 3

AMAZED IN GOD'S PRESENCE

I *used to think that the closer I got to the Lord, the less I needed*
people in my life. Exactly the opposite is true. The closer we
walk to the Lord, the more we see the need for support from
and accountability to other people. As the angel vanished, Mary
made a decision. She would visit Elizabeth and Zechariah. Mary
knew that Elizabeth would be the one person to offer her
support and encouragement. When the angels leave, when the
thrill of saying yes to God passes and we are in the difficult
places of obedience, we need people. The problem we have is
that we usually choose to get close to people who are on the
same level as we are spiritually (or a little lower), so we are rarely
challenged to live a more committed life. It was a mark of
Mary's maturity that she recognized her need for Elizabeth's
companionship and counsel. Mary *needed* Elizabeth, an older,
wiser friend.

As soon as Mary entered Elizabeth's house, remarkable things began to happen.[1] At Mary's shout of greeting, Elizabeth's unborn baby (later named John), leaped in her womb (Luke 1:41). Any mother will tell you that it's not unusual for a baby to move during pregnancy. But Elizabeth knew by a special work of the Holy Spirit that this movement on this occasion was no ordinary flutter. She said to Mary, "As soon as the sound of your greeting reached my ears, the baby in my womb leaped for *joy*" (v. 44).

God the Spirit also revealed to Elizabeth that Mary was to be the mother of the Messiah. Elizabeth uttered an amazing prophecy: "Blessed are you among women and blessed is the child you will bear! But why am I so favored, that the mother of my Lord should come to me? . . . Blessed is she who has believed that what the Lord has said to her will be accomplished!" (Luke 1:42-43, 45).

One of the great debates that rocked the early church was over what title to give Mary. In the fifth century at the Council of Ephesus, certain segments of the church wanted to give Mary the title *theotokos*, "mother of God."[2] Originally the title was a reflection on Mary's *son*; it was a declaration that Jesus was fully divine. Some of the church fathers at that council, however, saw the possibility that the title would be used to focus more attention on Mary. They thought that such a title would give Mary a more exalted place in the plan of redemption. Already in popular belief, people lifted Mary from her humble place as God's servant and propelled her to a status closer to deity. Mary is still addressed as "the Mother of God" by the Roman Catholic and Orthodox churches. The Bible, however, never gives her that title. I think we are on better biblical footing to refer to Mary as Elizabeth did—as "the mother of my Lord"—or simply as the mother of Jesus. Mary's child was God, but Mary was merely the vessel through which God the Son became flesh.

Mary's Song

John, still unborn, recognized Jesus, also unborn. Elizabeth recognized Mary as the mother of the promised Redeemer. Now Mary turns her heart toward God and speaks one of the most beautiful hymns ever heard. The Gospel writer Luke had a deep appreciation for the early hymns of praise and adoration to God. He saw to it that not only Mary's song but Zechariah's burst of praise (Luke 1:67-79) and Simeon's song of blessing (Luke 2:29-32) were preserved for our enjoyment and blessing.

Mary's song is sometimes called the "Magnificat." In the Latin version of the Bible used for hundreds of years in the medieval church, the word *magnificat* (which means "magnifies"or, as the NIV translates it, "glorifies") is the first word of the text. Probably no other words of Scripture (except Psalm 23) have been put to music more often than Mary's words of exaltation and glory to God. If you are somewhere other than on a crowded subway or in the reading room of the library, you may want to read these words out loud—or even sing the words as a spontaneous expression of praise offered to God:

My soul glorifies the Lord
   and my spirit rejoices in God my Savior,
for he has been mindful
   of the humble state of his servant.
From now on all generations will call me blessed,
   for the Mighty One has done great things for me—
   holy is his name.
His mercy extends to those who fear him,
   from generation to generation.
He has performed mighty deeds with his arm;
   he has scattered those who are proud in their inmost
      thought.
He has brought down rulers from their thrones
   but he has lifted up the humble.

He has filled the hungry with good things
   but has sent the rich away empty.
He has helped his servant Israel,
   remembering to be merciful
to Abraham and his descendants forever,
   even as he said to our fathers. (Luke 1:46-55)

I'm impressed with several things about Mary as I listen to her words. First I'm impressed with her knowledge of the Bible. She skillfully weaves together line after line of quotation or allusion to the Old Testament. In my own study of the song I've traced at least twenty-two lines from the Scriptures that Mary puts together to form a profoundly moving expression of trust in God. Those familiar with the Old Testament will hear echoes from Hannah's song of rejoicing when God allowed her to conceive her son, Samuel (1 Samuel 2:1-5). Even the form of Mary's song parallels the great psalms of Israel. Mary sings back to God the truths about him that she has learned in her study and meditation on his Word.

As I read this song, I'm also impressed with Mary's knowledge of the character and work of God. Mary not only knew her Bible; she also knew her Lord. The song is not about Mary or even directly about Jesus; it's about God, the deliverer of his people. No fewer than sixteen times Mary refers to the Lord God by name, title or appropriate pronoun *(he, him* or *his)*. More significantly, Mary marks out a number of God's attributes as objects of praise. She knew what God is like. In Luke 1:49 Mary calls God "the Mighty One," a reference to his power, his ability to do whatever he purposes to do. God's people or God's servants may be weak, but they have a mighty God. In the same verse she declares God's holiness—"holy is his name." Everything about God is holy, absolutely set apart from evil or deception. Other aspects of God's character equally praiseworthy are his mercy (v. 50), his justice (vv. 51-53) and his unwavering faithfulness (vv. 54-55).

After a long time of neglect, evangelical Christians have begun to focus their attention on worship. Hymns and choir music used to be seen simply as "filler" before the sermon. We've finally reconnected with a truth that many of our brothers and sisters in other traditions have known all along: Worship and praise to God deserve our time and our best.

Those of us who plan worship services or minister to other believers in music have a lot to learn from Mary's beautiful expression of worship to God. For example, what I feel or what I happen to think about certain issues may make wonderful songs sung for pleasure or entertainment or even encouragement. But songs sung in worship should be based on the solid declarations of God's Word. Above all, we should write or sing our songs of worship in such a way that the one exalted is God—not the singer or songwriter but the One to whom our worship is directed. The "style" of the music doesn't have much to do with it. I've heard African Christians praise God in jubilant worship that involved drums, shouts, handclapping and dance. On the other hand, I've witnessed some of the great old hymns sung in a spirit of pride and self-centeredness that brought some glory to the singer but little glory to God. We look at the outside; God looks at the heart. I have sung praise and worship choruses with a cold heart toward God, and I have been moved to tears of love by the same choruses sung with a heart of tenderness toward him. One of the most moving experiences I've ever had was standing with more than sixty thousand Promise Keepers in the Hoosier Dome singing, "Holy, Holy, Holy." There was no accompaniment, no soloist, no band—just one Audience and sixty thousand men singing the perfections of God's character.

God at Work
Mary's song also picks up several biblical themes that demon-

strate how God works in our world and in our lives. Mary is careful, for example, to emphasize the overshadowing, overpowering purpose of her life to bring glory to God—"My soul glorifies the Lord" (Luke 1:46). Mary's song rings with pure adoration. She exalts and honors God simply for who he is.

Mary extols the grace of God too. The Lord has at last vindicated the hopes and prayers of his people by choosing her to be the one through whom the promised Messiah would come. Mary is living proof that God is in the habit of showing his kindness not to those who think they deserve it but to those who humbly honor him. Twenty centuries later we are still impressed with Mary's deep sense of gratitude to God for the gracious favor he so lavishly poured out on her.

Mary also had a profound grasp of God's sovereign control over human history. She lived in a world ruled by the strong and the cruel. Even in Israel's worship, religious parties tried to impose the bondage of human tradition on the people. But God was about to turn the normal order of things upside down. He would scatter the proud and bring down rulers while he exalted the people no one noticed very much. The typical humble believer in Mary's day, just like typical, humble believers today, longed for God to set things right in justice and mercy. The poor find compassion in God's new order of things; the hungry are filled; the proud and the rich have to go to the end of the line for a change.

We can hear reverberations of Mary's hymn in the words of her son more than thirty years later:

Blessed are the poor in spirit. . . . Blessed are the meek. . . .
Blessed are those who hunger and thirst for righteousness,
for they will be filled. (Matthew 5:3-6)

In God's kingdom everything changes.

Mary's song links the ancient promises of God with the power of God to fulfill those promises. The hopes of hundred of generations were being satisfied in one blinding flash. David's messianic psalms looked forward with longing to the coming Deliverer; Mary's messianic hymn announces that God is about to keep his word.

Making It Personal

What impresses me most about Mary's song, however, is not her intense words or the powerful expressions of biblical truth. What impresses me most is that Mary knew her own need. At the end of Luke 1:46 Mary calls God her Savior. Was Mary sinless and above fallen humanity? No, Mary needed a Savior too! Mary was saved by putting her faith in her own son, Jesus Christ.

Mary would be called "blessed" by every generation because of the One who blessed her. Mary would be congratulated by uncounted Christians not simply as a passive example of what God can do through the most insignificant of people (humanly speaking) but more pointedly as an active model of a believer's obedient response to God.

God continues to look for men and women like Mary. God can take an unknown person who has a heart for him and can raise that person in grace to a place of enormous spiritual impact. Mary is the proof. God's plan isn't completed yet, so he is still looking for people who are humble enough to give him all the glory. Great works from God's hand and for his honor still wait to be done, and God waits too. He waits for a willing heart.

Chapter 4

A HUSBAND'S LOVE

*T*he list of names appears in our local newspaper once a week. Just below the names of those born and those who died are the names of couples filing for divorce. Maybe your name has been on that list. Certainly you have had a family member or friend who has gone through the pain of a broken marriage.

It's pretty shocking to open the pages of Scripture and find one of the Bible's heroes contemplating divorce. But when Joseph of Nazareth makes his first appearance in the biblical story, that's exactly what he is doing. His marriage to Mary has only been promised. The engagement period has already lasted a number of months, but now new information has come to light—information that crushes Joseph's heart and drives him to desperate extremes.

Maybe this is how the scene unfolded. Shortly after Mary's return from her visit with Elizabeth, she met Joseph in the garden of her parents' home or some other suitable location and told him that she was "with child." She told Joseph not with tears of shame but with quiet confidence. At first, Joseph couldn't believe what he was hearing. He even entertained the thought that Mary was joking with him, but he knew Mary would never joke in such a coarse way. What she said was true. She was pregnant.

Joseph's first question was the one any man would ask in the same situation: Who was the father? Joseph's conscience was clear. He had never violated the purity of the engagement period. His relationship with Mary had been carried out in full view of her family and the close-knit community surrounding them. But Mary obviously had not been the person Joseph thought she was. One of the things that had attracted Joseph to Mary was her humble desire to live transparently before her God and before the community of believers around her. But now, in one brief conversation, Joseph found his perception of Mary shattered—and his life in shambles.

When Joseph asked her who the father was, Mary said that an angel of God had spoken to her and told her that she would conceive miraculously. Her son would be the promised Deliverer, the Messiah, God's Son. She said it so calmly, confidently. But how could Joseph believe a story like that? He left the garden without saying another word and went back to his home to cry. He wrestled for hours with his response. Divorce seemed his only solution.

Local opinion would be harsh; most people would tell him to divorce her openly in a public condemnation before the religious leaders. That would bring Mary shame and reproach—or worse. In the old days, before the restrictions of Roman law, an adulteress was stoned. This *was* adultery, even though the marriage had not been consummated, for in Jewish custom the betrothal period began with the exchange of solemn vows as binding as those of a modern wedding ceremony.

The other option for Joseph was a private divorce. Two or three trusted friends would stand by as witnesses. Joseph would write out a bill of divorce and give it to Mary. No reason for the divorce needed to be mentioned; the community would find out only when people recognized that Joseph and Mary no longer sat together in the courtyard. They would also see Mary's figure begin to change as her unborn child grew to maturity.

As Joseph turned the options over and over in his mind, one fact emerged with such power that it overshadowed all his pain and sense of betrayal. Joseph realized that he loved Mary more than any other person he had ever known. He couldn't pay back her betrayal with more betrayal. Public humiliation was out of the question. He decided to divorce her privately and to do it quickly. He would arrange it the next day, and before the coming sabbath it would be completed. He would go on in life alone.

With that decision made, Joseph fell into an exhausted sleep. But in a dream God opened up to Joseph an option he had never considered. That's how God often works in our lives. When we are at the end of possibilities, the Lord opens a door that calls for a radical change of direction—and confident trust in God alone.

The Man Mary Loved

Both Mary and Joseph came from families who originally lived in the southern region of Palestine around Jerusalem. Both were descendants of David and traced their heritage to the clan of Judah, one of the sons of Jacob. Two genealogies of Jesus are listed in the New Testament. The genealogy in Matthew (1:1-17) traces Joseph's lineage from Abraham, the great father of Israel, through David and Solomon, the great kings of Israel.

Joseph stood in the royal line of David's descendants. The crushing destruction of Jerusalem and the long exile in Babylon almost six hundred years earlier had brought an end to the rule of Davidic kings, but Joseph stood in a very prestigious heritage. Jesus, as Joseph's "adopted" son, inherited all the privileges of royalty.

The second genealogy of Jesus recorded in Luke's Gospel most likely traces Jesus' heritage through Mary, his mother. Luke follows Mary's line back to David not through Solomon but through another of David's sons, Nathan. Then Luke goes all the way back to Abraham and beyond to Adam. Jesus through Joseph was the royal heir of David's kingdom, but through Mary Jesus was a member of the human race. He really was one of us!

It's possible that the forebears of Joseph and Mary were part of a migration of Jews from southern Judea up into the non-Jewish, pagan region of Galilee. That migration began in the time of the Hasmonaean king Aristobulus I, one hundred years before Jesus' birth. Zealous Jews around Jerusalem came to Galilee as missionaries to convert the non-Jews in the area to the worship of the true God—and they were successful. In Jesus' day Galilee was definitely a Jewish area, though it was still regarded as uncultured by the sophisticated Jews in Judea.

Joseph certainly inherited the spiritual zeal of the preceding generations. Matthew refers to Joseph as a "righteous man" (Matthew 1:19), and Luke portrays both Mary and Joseph as careful observers of the Law of Moses. Joseph was a carpenter, a trade he also taught to Jesus. In Mark 6:3 the people of Nazareth refer to Jesus as "the carpenter." The work of a carpenter was to plan and build homes, manufacture household furniture and construct farming tools. Joseph was not a wealthy man, but he should not be thought of as illiterate or untaught. The Jews expected every man to learn some occupation, and they placed high value on manual labor as a spiritual work offered to God. The great rabbis of Israel supported themselves with work. The trade of a carpenter ranked fairly high in the social structure. The prominent first-century rabbi Shammai was a carpenter, and his rival Hillel was a woodcutter. The apostle Paul, who from all indications came from a wealthy family and who was trained as a rabbi and scholar, also learned the trade of tentmaking (Acts 18:3).

Joseph is never mentioned as being present after Jesus' ministry begins thirty years after his birth in Bethlehem (Luke 3:23). Most scholars believe that Joseph had died by that time. That fact has prompted many students of the Bible to believe that Joseph was significantly older than Mary. Some even suggest that when Joseph wed Mary he was a widower who already had grown children from an earlier marriage. The biblical testimony, however, doesn't give us any hint about his age. It seems just as probable that Joseph was a young man, of an acceptable age for a young woman like Mary, but a man who was mature in his faith and trust in the Lord God.

An Angel's Visit

Joseph was privileged to receive three messages directly from an angel of God. On the first occasion, just after he had decided to divorce Mary privately, Joseph was visited by an angel in a dream. He didn't dream this up; it really happened while Joseph slept. The angel told Joseph that Mary's story was true. She was carrying the Messiah in her body. She had not been unfaithful to Joseph. The conception was a miraculous work of God; the child was God himself in human flesh.

In his carefully worded account of Joseph's experience, Matthew adds one more confirmation of Jesus' supernatural conception. He reaches back into the ancient prophecies of Isaiah and finds a stirring prediction: "All this took place to fulfill what the Lord had said through the prophet: 'A virgin will be with child and will give birth to a son, and they will call him Immanuel'—which means, 'God with us' " (Matthew 1:22-23).

I spoke to several hundred university students one Christmas about the birth of Jesus. I tried to get them to see beyond the sentimentalism of the story as they had heard it for so many years and to focus on the wonder of Jesus' coming as a human being. After I spoke, one student said, "I believe Jesus was God, but I don't think this whole story of a virgin birth is really that important. What difference does it make if Jesus was Joseph's son—or some other man's?"

He asked a serious question, and it deserved a serious answer. Theologians have usually argued that the virgin conception was necessary because it "proved" certain things about Jesus. Some Bible teachers have claimed, for example, that the virgin conception was necessary to guarantee that Jesus would not inherit a sinful human nature. The apostle Paul seems to indicate that (at least in a theological sense) our sinful nature is passed to us from Adam through our fathers. But Jesus could have inherited a sinful human nature from his mother, since men and women are equally fallen as a result of Adam's sin. This same desire to somehow protect Jesus from inherited sin led to the belief in the immaculate conception of Mary. If we believe that Mary was without sin, then Jesus clearly was sinless since he could not have inherited a sinful nature from his father *or* his mother. The New Testament, however, seems to avoid that argument completely. The angel simply says that the Holy Spirit would overshadow the entire event and, because of the Spirit's protection, Mary's offspring would be holy (Luke 1:35).

Another theological argument sometimes advanced for the necessity of the virgin conception is that it demonstrates Jesus' preexistence. If Jesus had been conceived by a man and a woman, he would have begun to exist at his conception. The fact is, however, that God the Son has always existed, and his entrance into the world of humanity required a virgin conception. Jesus did not begin to exist in Mary's womb; Jesus became flesh in Mary's womb.

No orthodox Christian would deny that God the Son had existed from eternity. Before Mary was born, before Abraham or David existed, before the worlds were made, the Son was in existence. But God could have brought about the incarnation by any one of the possible ways that his infinite mind could have conceived. Out of all the possibilities, God the Son became human through a virgin conception in Mary.

The virgin conception does not necessarily *prove* anything about who Jesus was. It is consistent with other biblical truths, but it doesn't prove that Jesus was God or eternal or sinless. What is at stake in the virgin conception is not so much our understanding of Christ but our confidence in the Scriptures. If Jesus was conceived in Mary by Joseph or by any other man, the Bible (at least at this point) is a lie. Those who reject the virgin conception because it seems embarrassing in our scientific age have thrown away their confidence in the Bible as the truth of God.

When I finished my long defense of the virgin conception, the student who asked the question was undaunted. "But if you read the myths of the ancient world, you can find other so-called virgin birth stories. Maybe Luke just borrowed the idea from other cultures in order to spice up the story a little." In my own undergraduate days I had confronted the same argument, and it led me on a search for these other virgin-birth stories. What I found were two kinds of miraculous birth stories.

Most were stories like the birth of Hercules, who was the child of the Greek god Zeus and a human woman. These accounts involved a sexual encounter between a god and a human woman. If the woman was a virgin before the encounter, she was not considered a virgin afterward. The so-called virgin birth stories almost always involved some kind of sexual encounter between a god or goddess and a human being, an element totally absent from the biblical account. A few other pagan stories were like the Greek myth of the birth of Alexander the Great. The story goes that Alexander was virgin born after his mother, Olympia, cohabited with a serpent! It's a crude story doubtlessly derived from mythological stories about a powerful man, most likely long after his death.

Obviously, neither type of so-called virgin birth myth can compare with the holiness and wonder of the historical record of Jesus' miraculous conception in Mary found in the Bible.

In my first pastorate a doctor in our congregation, the obstetrician who delivered our two oldest children, gave a presentation one Sunday evening about how human life begins and develops over the first nine months of life. He started with a projected picture of a fertilized human egg, magnified hundreds of times. I will never forget his words as we looked at that picture. "This," he said, "is the degree to which Jesus Christ humbled himself to come to earth to be our Savior." Jesus came not as a glorious being descending from heaven in radiant splendor, not as a king born to great acclaim, not even at first as a baby lying in a manger. The infinite God, the Creator of the universe, became a tiny human embryo in Mary. By that act, Jesus stepped down into time and space. He identified himself irreversibly with his own creatures and his own creation.

Making It Personal

Joseph demonstrated his righteous character by responding to the angel's message with immediate obedience. Joseph obeyed God's word whether it was written in the Law of Moses or spoken in a dream by an angel. His obedience made a marriage where there might have been a divorce. The tears of bitterness he had shed the night before turned into shouts of joy in the morning. Joseph and Mary took the final vows of marriage, and Joseph took Mary to his own home. No consummation of the marriage took place until after Jesus was born, but Mary's companionship was an immediate, satisfying reality in Joseph's life.

God the Father delivered his own Son into the home of two people whose hearts were fully his. Reading Joseph's story makes me wonder what risks I am willing to take to be fully obedient to the will of God. Those of us who want to experience "life on the edge" will never come closer to the edge than when we take the risk of pursuing the options that God opens to us.

The whole story of Jesus' birth is a story of trust—Mary had to trust God's promise, Joseph had to trust Mary, later Mary had to trust Joseph as they fled from Herod's slaughter. Trust is difficult because it leaves us vulnerable. If we trust our mate and our mate fails us or deceives us, we look foolish. If we trust God and things don't seem to work out right, we feel embarrassed. Joseph must have wondered in times of difficulty if his encounter with the angel had been real. But as he walked on, trusting God at each step, he learned that God could be trusted.

Not one direct word from Joseph is recorded anywhere in the Bible. Most of the people involved in the story of Jesus' birth talked or sang or shouted in praise, but not Joseph. He obeyed. Quietly, courageously, with the tenderness of a father, he demonstrated his faith by risking everything to obey the Lord. Mary had been promised to the right man! Both were willing to give up their reputations if that was what God asked of them.

Chapter 5

DUSTING OFF
THE NATIVITY SET

I *wonder if Mary ever worried about the kind of world she was* bringing a child into. Being born in first-century Palestine would be like being born today in some tense, war-ravaged area of our world. Violence and extortion were a way of life. Evil dictators and petty warlords conspired together to terrorize the population and to squeeze every dime from increasingly oppressed people. Any word of protest was met with a bludgeon—or a cross.

When Luke, the Gospel writer, begins to tell the story of Jesus' birth, the first person he mentions is not Mary or Joseph or the shepherds. The headliner in Luke's script is Caesar Augustus: "In those days Caesar Augustus issued a decree that a census should be taken of the entire Roman world" (Luke 2:1). In the eyes of the average citizen, Caesar Augustus was the supreme ruler, the *imperator,* the emperor over the vast empire of Rome. His personal name was Gaius Octavius; his aristocratic credentials were impeccable. His rise to power began in 44 B.C., when his mother's uncle, Julius Caesar, was assassinated. To the surprise of nearly everyone, the nineteen-year-old Octavius, who had been serving as one of Caesar's staff officers, was named sole heir in Caesar's will. Those who laughed at the thought of an untried boy in a position of leadership over the Roman world soon discovered that Octavius was a cunning, ambitious and exceptionally cruel young man. Octavius and his ally Marc Antony brought bloody vengeance on his great uncle's murderers. Then Octavius turned on Antony and emerged in 31 B.C. as the sole ruler of the Roman Empire.

The Senate, in gratitude for the peace he had restored to a battered empire, heaped honors and power on Octavius. They proclaimed him emperor ("Caesar") and gave him the title Augustus, which evoked reverential awe and authority. The Senate and people of Rome gave him unhindered control over the affairs of the empire. He was a god.

At the time of Jesus' birth, the Roman Empire encompassed nearly 55 million people and stretched from the English Channel through present-day Europe to the lands of the eastern Mediterranean and Egypt back across north Africa to Spain. In the eyes of those living in the empire, Rome controlled virtually the entire civilized world.

All of this political intrigue would have affected Mary and Joseph very little if sixty years earlier (in 64 B.C.) the Roman general Pompey had not conquered Asia Minor and forced the kingdoms around the eastern Mediterranean, including Judea and Galilee, to acknowledge Roman authority. In time the Jewish rulers in Palestine were replaced by puppet-kings, most notably Herod the Great in 37 B.C. As a result, when Caesar Augustus decided that the entire Roman world should submit to a census, everyone in Herod's kingdom, including Joseph of Nazareth in Galilee, was forced to comply. A decree from Rome could not be ignored, even if the emperor lived fifteen hundred miles away.

Augustus had several reasons for ordering a census. An enrollment would give the emperor some idea of how many male Roman citizens lived in the empire. Augustus was deeply disturbed by a decline in marriage and birth rates among the official citizens of Rome and a corresponding increase in births among subject people and slaves. He was even known to lecture groups of single Roman men who were loitering around the forum. He passionately reminded them of their responsibility to raise up legitimate descendants for the glory of Rome![1]

Caesar's enrollment also pushed the noses of the empire's conquered peoples down into Roman authority. As much as they resented this intrusion into their lives and as inconvenient as the census requirements might be, noncitizens had no choice but to obey the Roman decree.

The most useful function of the census was taxation. The "IRS" was around in the first century too! Running an empire requires money, and Caesar Augustus wanted everyone's contribution. So a decree went out that everyone in the Roman world should register at the city of their ancestral family's origin.

I don't think Mary and Joseph understood until later that behind the decision of the earthly sovereign in Rome stood a sovereign God working out his eternal plan. God used a man like Caesar Augustus to sign a decree affecting the whole empire so that one little prophecy tucked away in a forgotten Old Testament book would be perfectly fulfilled. That's how serious God is about his promises. Six hundred fifty years before Caesar signed that imperial order, God had moved a prophet named Micah to write that the Messiah would be born in David's city of Bethlehem (Micah 5:2). Mary and Joseph lived in Nazareth of Galilee, eighty miles north by the straight route from Bethlehem, ninety miles by the more traditional route along the Jordan River. God saw to it that a decree issued from Rome would cause an unknown man and his pregnant wife to travel to Bethlehem just in time so that Jesus would be born where God had said he would be born. Caesar, strutting around in Rome, thought the census was *his* idea, but it was God moving in human history to fulfill his own Word. Caesar Augustus thought *he* was in control, but he wasn't.

Mary was probably not required to go to Bethlehem with Joseph. The thought of a four- or five-day journey at her advanced stage of pregnancy was certainly not very appealing. But the thought of being all alone at the time of Jesus' birth was a possibility Mary refused to consider. The picture of Joseph leading a donkey on which Mary sits is enshrined in the art and literature of Christianity. Nothing is said in Scripture, however, about a donkey. In their relative poverty it is questionable whether Joseph even owned a donkey. On a donkey's back or on foot, the journey would have been difficult and exhausting, and when they arrived in the small village of Bethlehem, the inn built to house traveling pilgrims was full.

Away in a Manger

That there was "no room in the inn" for a tired, obviously pregnant woman sounds very unfair until you understand what the inns were like. Rural inns in the first century were not Holiday Inns or Red Roof Inns! They were not much more than a large room sheltered by four walls and a roof. The center of the room was designed to house the animals of the people who lodged there. Around the perimeter of the room a low platform was built for the people to sleep on. There were no beds, no privacy. Families simply slept where they could find room. The inn was crowded and noisy.

It was probably a compassionate innkeeper or his tender wife who directed Mary and Joseph to the stable behind the inn. If tradition is correct, the stable was simply a cave, one of many that perforate the hills around Bethlehem. In the quiet and privacy of that stable, Mary gave birth to a son.

Two thousand years have made very few changes in Bethlehem. Compared to the larger cities around it, Bethlehem is still a small town, six miles southwest of Jerusalem. Manger Square dominates the center of the city and leads any visitor to the ancient Church of the Nativity. Constantine, the first Christian emperor of Rome, had the original church built in A.D. 326 over the cave earlier identified as the birthplace of Jesus by the early church fathers Origen (A.D. 185-254) and Justin Martyr (A.D. 100-165). A stairway leads down to a small cavern under the high altar of the church. The cavern, called the Grotto of the Nativity, is supposed to be the spot where Jesus was born. A silver star on the floor is inscribed with these words: "HIC DE VIRGINE MARIA JESUS CHRISTUS NATUS EST" (Latin for "Here Jesus Christ was born of the virgin Mary").[2]

Unfortunately we have romanticized this scene in Bethlehem. We've painted the stable in the warm golden glow of a Christmas card. In reality it was pretty dreadful. Imagine coming upon a young woman giving birth to a baby in an abandoned car in some urban alleyway and you come closer to the way it really was. I've never been in a cave—or a stable—that looked or smelled like a place I would want to sleep.

It strikes me too that even though Mary and Joseph had some privacy in that stable, they were also all alone. At a time when Mary needed help and care as at no other time in a woman's life, no one was there to help except faithful Joseph. No member of Mary's family had traveled with them; apparently no midwife came to help. Luke, the gentle physician, is careful to say that *Mary* gave birth to the child. *She* wrapped him in strips of cloth to comfort and warm him. *She* laid him in the manger. *She* did it (Luke 2:7). Mary is a young woman and Jesus is her first child, but she did it all herself.

When God came to earth, he bypassed the palace of Caesar Augustus and the chambers of the temple. He came into this world poor and lonely and virtually unnoticed. Maybe that is how you feel as you read these lines. Maybe you are gripped by sorrow or loss or loneliness. You may be out of work or out of hope. I want you to know that when God came to earth for you, he came lower than you are right now. You may think that nobody cares and that nobody understands your situation, but you are mistaken. Our God knows what it's like in the pit of despair. He has been there.

"Shepherds, Why This Jubilee?"

In contrast to the loneliness and poverty of the birth in the stable, a scene of incredible glory was unfolding outside the town of Bethlehem. Luke 2:8-9 tells us that some shepherds were out that night, guarding their flocks, when suddenly an angel of the Lord stood at their campsite. His brilliance blazed in the night sky, and the poor shepherds were scared to death. The angel said, "Don't be afraid!" Why not be afraid? Who wouldn't be afraid? "I bring you good news," the angel continued, "of great joy that will be for all the people. Today in the town of David a Savior has been born to you; he is Christ the Lord."

That announcement did not come to Caesar Augustus or to the high priest of Israel. The angel did not burst in on worshipers in prayer in the temple. He came instead to men on a hillside who had hearts open enough to receive the message.

The angel gave them a sign. The Savior would be wrapped in strips of cloth (not unusual for a newborn) but would be lying in a manger (highly unusual). Those shepherds knew exactly where to look in Bethlehem. They were very familiar with animal pens. They scoured every stable until they found Mary and Joseph—and the Savior.

But before they left the hillside to go to Bethlehem, with the angel's words still ringing in their ears, suddenly the whole sky exploded with light and sound as a multitude of angels praised God. "Glory to God in the highest, and on earth peace to men on whom his favor rests" (Luke 2:14). The world may not have noticed this child born in a stable, but heaven couldn't be silent. The angelic hosts of heaven shouted the story.

As suddenly as the angels had come, they left. And as soon as one of the shepherds found voice enough to speak, he said, "Let's go to Bethlehem and see." In the stable behind the traveler's inn they found Mary and Joseph and the marvelous baby.

Making It Personal

How can we respond to this incredible event? I realize that the Christian community celebrates Christmas every year, but if you are like me our Christmas observance always seems inadequate. More often than we would like to admit, our declaration that "Jesus is the reason for the season" is contradicted by our frantic activity and obsessive concern with gifts. So how can we genuinely celebrate Jesus' birth? And how can we extend our joy about God coming to earth beyond a few weeks in December? We can find some suggestions on how to celebrate Christ's birth in Luke's Gospel, in the verses we usually skip over when we are reading the story.

One suggestion comes from the shepherds who saw the baby and then went out to spread the word. They became witnesses! They had heard the angels' song; they had seen the Savior, the Lord. How could they remain silent? They had good news to tell, just like we do. The shepherds knew their world desperately needed to hear their message, just as our world does. One way to celebrate Christ's coming is to imitate the shepherds in spreading the word about Jesus Christ.

Another way to keep the joy of Christ's coming alive in our hearts is by being amazed at it. The people who heard the shepherds' story were amazed at what they heard (Luke 2:18). I think most of us have lost that sense of wonder and awe. We've heard the story so many times that we yawn our way through it. But the fact that the Lord of glory stepped down into human time and space to be our Savior ought to cause us to be amazed, to be filled with holy wonder.

Mary's reflection on both Jesus' birth and the shepherds' visit gives us another biblical response to this wonderful event. "Mary treasured up all these things and pondered them in her heart" (Luke 2:19). Amazement and wonder produce the fruit of meditation, what Luke calls "pondering." Meditation is the devotion of time to think carefully and deeply about what God has done. It involves the mind *and* the emotions. Mary treasured the events in her heart. It's as if every time she thought about what had happened and its significance, she would take out a valuable jewel and turn it over and over, admiring its beauty, losing herself in contemplation. Meditation is another lost spiritual discipline for most of us. We live at such a frenzied pace that we rarely stop long enough to think carefully about God's marvelous works in our lives. You are probably reading this chapter with several other things on your mind that you could be doing or should be doing. One profitable way to keep the joy of Christ's coming vibrantly alive in our hearts is to spend some time remembering God's works and then using those memories to warm our affections for the Lord.

A stirred mind and a warm heart of devotion will prompt another response to Christ's birth. Our hearts will overflow in words of praise to God. The feelings of love in our hearts find expression in the words that we speak to him or sing to him in adoration and worship. The shepherds "returned, glorifying and praising God for all the things they had heard and seen" (Luke 2:20). I've always been impressed that the shepherds did not go to church to praise and glorify God. They returned. They went back to their sheep—to their jobs, to their homes. It's wonderful to lift our voices together in worship in church or in a small group, but the real secret to keeping the joy of Christmas ringing in our hearts and motivating our lives is to learn to praise and glorify God wherever we are.

Maybe that is how you can conclude this chapter. Not by charging off to do the things that have pressed themselves on your mind while you have been reading but by taking a few quiet minutes to think about God's wonderful grace and goodness in your life. Write some things down that are sources of wonder. Then turn them over as you would a treasure and allow God's Spirit to fill your heart with love and adoration. When your heart is full, pour out a sacrifice of praise to God. Let him know how you feel about him. You may find your job on the hillside today transformed from drudgery or frantic busyness to an unbelievable opportunity to let others know about the wonderful Savior who has come.

Chapter 6

HOLDING GOD
IN OUR ARMS

*Most of us are familiar with "The Twelve Days of Christ-*mas." Sometime every December you probably find yourself singing, "Three French hens, two turtledoves and a partridge in a pear tree." Several years ago at a high-school choir concert I heard another song called "The Twelve Days *After* Christmas." The female vocalist told us how on the first day after Christmas she and her true love had a fight. Things went downhill from there. The pear tree was chopped down, the seven swans drowned, the five golden rings turned her fingers green, and the three French hens became chicken soup!

That song gives a different slant to the sweet Christmas song we are familiar with. The same is true of the Christmas story. We know it very well. But I wonder if we are as familiar with what happened one week or one month after Jesus was born. We tend to leave Mary and Joseph and Jesus in the stable, and we forget what happened next.

It is not surprising that Mary and Joseph stayed in Bethlehem after Jesus was born. Mary needed time to recover from both the exhausting journey from Nazareth and the even more exhausting effort of giving birth. Most likely Joseph's trade as a carpenter provided income, and the quiet village provided an opportunity to rest. Bethlehem was also close to Jerusalem and the temple, and the temple would play an important part in what happened to Jesus and his parents in the weeks that followed his birth.

The Law of Moses placed three requirements on Mary and Joseph when Jesus was born. First, on the eighth day after his birth, Jesus was to be circumcised. Circumcision was the sign that a child was part of God's covenant people (Genesis 17:10-12). A priest or rabbi or even the child's father would perform the circumcision with great praise to God. This occasion was also the time when the child was officially named. Joseph and Mary obeyed the angel of God and named the boy Jesus, "the Lord saves" (Luke 2:21).

Thirty-two more days passed quietly in Bethlehem. The Law said that forty days after the birth of a male child, the mother was to offer a sacrifice at the temple for her purification (Leviticus 12:1-8). Because blood is involved in the act of giving birth, the woman was made ceremonially unfit to enter the temple for worship. Simply as a reminder of the curse of sin and of God's judgment on Eve which made pain part of the process of childbirth, sacrifices had to be made. The Law required two sacrifices—a lamb offered as a burnt offering and a dove or pigeon offered as a sin offering. If you were too poor to buy a lamb, the Law allowed the offering of two doves or pigeons. We get some insight into the poverty of Mary and Joseph when we read in Luke 2:24 that they offered two birds. They couldn't afford a lamb.

When the offering for purification had been made, when the fellowship between God and the worshiper had been symbolically restored, Mary and Joseph were ready to carry out the third requirement of the Law. They presented their first-born son to the Lord. The background of this custom lies in the deepest roots of Israel's story. We have to go back to the time of Moses, when God determined to deliver the people of Israel from their bondage in Egypt. The final plague God brought on Egypt was the death of the first-born throughout the land. The first-born lamb of every sheep and the first-born son of every Egyptian mother died in one dreadful night. The people of Israel escaped the plague because in obedience to God's Word they smeared the blood of a lamb on the doorposts of their houses. The angel of death passed over any home marked with blood.

Because he had delivered Israel with such a dramatic display of power, God claimed the first-born son in each family as his own possession (Exodus 13:2). That son belonged to God to serve as a priest before him. Later God set apart one family in Israel to be priests for the nation. The family of Aaron from the clan of Levi was chosen to conduct the worship of the people. God then allowed the families of Israel to redeem their first-born sons—in effect, to buy back the sons that belonged to God.

Here's how it worked. The parents came to the temple and handed their infant son to a priest. They were symbolically giving that child to God. By that act they acknowledged God's ownership. The priest lifted the child before the Lord and blessed God for his gracious gift. Then the parents paid the redemption price of five shekels and by that payment redeemed the child from the obligation of serving in the temple. The child was handed back to the parents as God's possession entrusted to them.

As Mary made her way into Jerusalem with her husband and her baby, she found herself surrounded by the noises and smells of a bustling city. She must have also been moved in her spirit by the splendor of the temple of the Lord. I talked this week with the mother of a six-week-old baby. She observed that Mary probably hadn't had a full night's sleep since the baby's birth. Mary may have been struggling with some depression or irritability (as this mother was). The last thing Mary may have *felt* like doing was going to church! But here she was, pulled along by her commitment to the Law and by a husband determined to finish what they had come to do.

Just as they were about to approach the priest, something totally unexpected happened. A man stepped out in front of them—an old man named Simeon—and, to Mary and Joseph's amazement, he blessed Jesus as God's Messiah.

Simeon's Psalm

We don't know much about Simeon. Luke doesn't tell us his occupation or where he lived or who his relatives were. We aren't told if he was rich or poor. Luke tells us the things about Simeon that were important to God.

First, Simeon was a believer in the Lord God; he was "righteous" (Luke 2:25). Simeon had come to trust in the God of Israel. In addition, Simeon was "devout"; he took his love for the Lord very seriously by observing the commands and requirements of the Law (Luke 2:25). The third thing Luke tells us about Simeon is that he was waiting—waiting for the consolation of Israel. That is an Old Testament way of saying that Simeon was looking for the Messiah. In those dark days of King Herod's brutality, at the end of four hundred years in which there had been no prophet sent from God to Israel, Simeon still believed that God would keep his promises to his people. God keeps his word even when things look worst. We often forget in a week or two the marvelous things that God has done in our lives. Simeon kept waiting.

Luke's final description of Simeon is that the Holy Spirit was upon this man. As you read the Old Testament you will find that phrase used to refer to a special anointing or empowering of the Holy Spirit poured out on chosen men and women.[1] The Spirit's anointing resulted in supernatural knowledge for Simeon. It had been revealed to him that he would see the Messiah before he died. We don't know how that knowledge was imparted to Simeon. He may have had a vision or a dream. The knowledge may have come to him as he studied the Old Testament prophecies, particularly Daniel 9, where God sets out a timetable for the Messiah's first coming. Somehow the Holy Spirit conveyed the truth to Simeon that he would not die until he had seen the Anointed One of God.

The empowering of the Holy Spirit on Simeon's life also resulted in divine guidance. Luke says that he came into the temple on this particular day "moved by the Spirit" (Luke 2:27). As Mary and Joseph brought Jesus into the courts of the temple to carry out the requirement of the Law, Simeon stepped out and took the baby in his arms. When he saw *this* couple with *this* baby, the Spirit whispered to his soul, "That's the one, Simeon. The baby is the Messiah of Israel."

Can you imagine how that must have felt? To wait for years, day after day, to go to the temple and watch and hear God say, "Not yet, Simeon, not yet." Now to be stopped in front of a poor, young couple and to have the longing of your heart fulfilled. "This one, Simeon, is the Christ!"

Some students of Luke's Gospel believe that Simeon was the priest who was responsible that day to bless those children who were brought to the temple. Luke doesn't say that, but whether Simeon was the priest or not, he certainly imitated the priest. He took Jesus in his hands—he held God in his arms—and he blessed the Lord. Praise sprang from his lips. Simeon uttered another of the stirring hymns that Luke is so careful to record:

Sovereign Lord, as you have promised,
you now dismiss your servant in peace.
For my eyes have seen your salvation,
which you have prepared in the sight of all people,
a light for revelation to the Gentiles
and for glory to your people Israel. (Luke 2:29-32)

Finish Well

"Finish well" is a piece of advice my father has often given me, usually when I was least interested in hearing it. When I left a job for a new one or finished work on a degree or completed mowing the lawn, Dad always stressed the importance of ending well. Simeon is a model for all of us who want to finish well. He didn't come to the end of his life and become a grumpy, self-centered old man. Instead, Simeon cultivated a tender heart to the Lord and to the people around him. He saw himself, in fact, as the Lord's servant. He begins his song of praise by using a very unusual word to refer to God; it's the Greek word from which we get the English word *despot*. It means "absolute master." Simeon gives God the highest place in his life, and he takes the lowest place. He calls himself God's "servant," literally, "bondslave."

Have you been keeping track of Simeon's spiritual credentials? So far we've seen his devotion of God, his trust in God's word, his anointing by God's Spirit and now his complete submission to God's authority. The world looks at wealth or power or fame to measure success and influence. God looks at the heart. God searches for men and women fully submitted to him.

Simeon is now ready to be dismissed in peace. He has waited to see the Messiah, and now he has seen God's salvation.

Simeon didn't know at that time how this six-week-old baby would accomplish deliverance for lost humanity, but he did know that the final plan had been set in motion by this single birth.

As he completes his song, Simeon is able to catch a glimpse of what this salvation will produce. The Spirit gives him the insight to see just a flash of God's new society. Simeon sees beyond the cross to the new age of the church. God has prepared this salvation with all people in view. The Messiah will be the glory of Israel, but he will also bring the light of God's truth to the Gentiles (Luke 2:32). We've had two thousand years to condition us to accept non-Jews in the program of God's grace, but that was a radical thought in Simeon's day. That God would ever reach out in love to Gentiles was unthinkable. But Simeon saw the new day coming.

Maybe that is what amazed Mary and Joseph. Obviously they knew that Jesus was the Messiah, but that Simeon would know—that was amazing! And that Jesus would provide salvation for the world was even *more* amazing!

A Sword in Mary's Soul

From blessing Jesus, Simeon now turns to blessing Mary and Joseph. From praising God, Simeon turns to predicting Jesus' success. Jesus, Simeon said, would be a divider in Israel. "This child is destined to cause the falling and rising of many in Israel, and to be a sign that will be spoken against, so that the thoughts of many hearts will be revealed" (Luke 2:34-35). Men and women will either rise or fall depending on their response to Jesus. People like Simeon who believe will be exalted; the majority of people by refusing to believe will be thrown down.

Then, almost as a whisper to Mary, Simeon predicts the sorrow that Mary will experience as Jesus' mother: "And a sword will pierce your own soul too." That prediction came true thirty-three years later at the foot of a cross on Calvary's hill. Mary, who held Jesus in her arms on this day, would watch him die. His suffering would slice into her soul like a sword.

At that very moment, a very old woman who lived continually in the temple came up and added her words of blessing and praise to God:

There was also a prophetess, Anna, the daughter of Phanuel, of the tribe of Asher. She was very old; she had lived with her husband seven years after her marriage, and then was a widow until she was eighty-four. She never left the temple but worshiped night and day, fasting and praying. Coming up to them at that very moment, she gave thanks to God and spoke about the child to all who were looking forward to the redemption of Jerusalem. (Luke 2:36-38)

Making It Personal

Simeon and Anna are minor characters in the story of God's redemption. They appear briefly on a page of Scripture and then are gone. They don't get much press when the Christmas story is told. But they stand as reminders to us, living two thousand years later, that God does not forget his people. Simeon was unknown as far as the world was concerned, an old man whose productivity was at an end. But he was greatly blessed of God. Anna probably was never written up on the society page of the *Jerusalem Post*, but she tasted the new age the Messiah would usher in.

Your Christian commitment, your trust in Christ and obedience to his Word, will not gain the world's applause. It won't bring wealth or fame or power, but God is the One who will settle the accounts. You may be very small in the world's estimation, with few abilities and fewer material resources. Maybe you, like Simeon and Anna, are old and unable to do much. God's word to us is to keep trusting him. His rewards will come.

Simeon and Anna also remind us to keep praising. In the press of the busyness of our lives, there should be the constant theme of praise. Praise is the distinctive mark of the genuine Christian life. God's love *for* us and God's faithfulness *to* us ought to overflow continually in praise.

Mary and Joseph must have left the temple that day with their heads spinning. God had pulled the curtain back a little more on his plan. What stretched ahead for this son of theirs seemed beyond belief.

Chapter 7

STRANGERS
AT THE DOOR

*W*e *three kings of Orient are;*
Bearing gifts, we traverse afar
Field and fountain, moor and mountain,
Following yonder star.

We sing that Christmas carol every year, and most of us believe
it! Most people believe that three kings or wise men, riding on
camels, came to the stable where Jesus was born and brought
gifts. Unfortunately, most of what we believe about the wise
men comes from the people who draw the pictures on Christmas cards, not from the Bible.

Many of the legends about the wise men have their roots in
the Middle Ages. According to medieval legend, there were
three wise men who were eastern kings. These men supposedly
represented the three main families of the human race, so one
is usually pictured as a black man, one as an east Asian and one

as a white European. They even have names—Caspar, Balthasar and Melchior. Several churches in Europe boast of having the bones or skull of one of the wise men.

None of these legends is biblical. What we can know for sure about the wise men is just what Matthew tells us and what we can glean from other reliable historical sources. Matthew simply says: "After Jesus was born in Bethlehem in Judea, during the time of King Herod, Magi from the east came to Jerusalem" (Matthew 2:1). The magi (or wise men in the King James Version) were a class of priests in Persia. They were not kings, but they held incredible political power. The Roman Empire had extended itself completely around the Mediterranean Sea. Judea and Jerusalem were on the eastern edges of the realm. Farther east, outside of Roman control but in almost constant warfare with Rome, loomed the old Persian or Parthian Empire. The magi were pagan priests of Parthia who were highly respected for their wisdom and for their political clout. No king ruled over the Parthian Empire without cultivating the favor of the magi.

The religion of the magi is pretty vague to us. The majority of the magi held to an early form of Zoroastrianism, a religion in which two gods, one good god and one evil god, constantly struggled for supremacy. Most of their theology was astrology. The magi believed that the stars and planets control our lives and the events of the world. They practiced fortunetelling, divining answers to difficult questions, and their greatest secret art, the interpretation of dreams. The name *magi* was later corrupted into the English word *magic* because of their preoccupation with weird, occult power.

Six hundred years before Jesus' birth, someone had joined the ranks of the magi who brought dramatic change in some of their lives. The young Jewish man Daniel was taken to Babylon by King Nebuchadnezzar to be trained in the language and culture of Babylon. Daniel became one of the magi. Because of God's blessing on his life, Daniel rose to a place of prominence over all the magi and for at least forty years held a position of great respect and power. Daniel's influence continued even after the Babylonians were conquered by the rising Persian Empire. From his position of leadership Daniel had remarkable impact on the magi. I am convinced that Daniel led some of the magi to faith in the true and living God. I'm just as convinced that he taught them from the Scriptures. He taught them that a Messiah would come from Israel and that he would be God's anointed Deliverer for all believing humanity. These same magi would have read Daniel's own writings in which God predicted that 483 years after the Jewish people were released from captivity, the Messiah would come (Daniel 9:25-26).

What we have in Matthew 2 are not pagan kings coming to find Jesus but believers in the true God seeking the promised Messiah. Some of the magi down through the six hundred years since Daniel had remained faithful to Daniel's God. Those magi who came to Jerusalem had waited and watched and prayed for the birth of the coming King, and now they were convinced that it had happened.

Herod's Trouble

When Herod looked out his window to see his newest guests gathered in the courtyard, he probably did not see three men climbing down from camels. The magi and the Parthian soldiers who accompanied them most likely rode magnificent Persian horses. Their arrival in Jerusalem sent shock waves through Herod. Three wars had already been fought between Rome and Parthia, and Judea had suffered the brunt of the battle. The Roman Empire was quiet at this time, but the emperor, Caesar Augustus, was old. Herod the Great had ruled Judea for almost forty years, but he was old too. The time seemed ripe for another Parthian invasion. What could be worse than to have powerful Parthian magi accompanied by a regiment of crack Parthian troops come to Jerusalem looking for a newborn king of the Jews!

Agitation spread from Herod's palace to the whole city. As soon as the magi dismounted, they began to ask the question they thought anyone in the city could answer. "Where is the one who has been born king of the Jews? We saw his star in the east and have come to worship him" (Matthew 2:2).

The "star" the magi saw has puzzled Bible students for two thousand years. Some say it was a new star that suddenly appeared; others say it was a comet or a rare alignment of planets. The word translated "star" is the Greek word *astera,* from which we get our English words *asteroid* and *astronomy.* It can refer to any cosmic body. I believe the biblical evidence points to a comet, because (as we will see) the "star" is not always in the sky but appears, then is gone and then reappears.

The magi studied the skies constantly. One night as these men watched the heavens, longing in their hearts for Daniel's Messiah to be born, suddenly a new phenomenon appeared. Their own testimony is "we saw *his* star in the east." The star was a sign that the Messiah had been born.

I wish a biblically aware CNN reporter had been on the scene asking questions, because what the magi don't tell us is how they connected the birth of the Messiah with the appearance of a new star in the heavens. Maybe they linked it to an ancient prophecy in Israel's Law:

I see him, but not now;
  I behold him, but not near.
A star will come out of Jacob;
  a scepter will rise out of Israel. . . .
A ruler will come out of Jacob. (Numbers 24:17, 19)

Somehow the Spirit of God revealed to these waiting hearts that the new king's birth was announced by that star.

The star did not, however, lead them to Jerusalem. They saw the star while they were still "in the east." They came to Jerusalem thinking that certainly someone in the center of Jewish life and worship would know where the new king had been born. But when they began to ask, no one knew. Finally word got to Herod, and the murderous old man was troubled. The people knew what kind of persecution Herod could unleash when his power was threatened. They were troubled because Herod was troubled.

Herod *did* know where to go for answers, however. He gathered the brain trust of Israel together and quickly got a response to his question. The Messiah, the anointed King of Israel, was to be born in Bethlehem of Judea. These religious leaders even quoted chapter and verse of their authority:

For this is what the prophet has written:
"But you, Bethlehem, in the land of Judah,
are by no means least among the rulers of Judah;
for out of you will come a ruler
who will be the shepherd of my people Israel."
(Matthew 2:5-6, quoting Micah 5:2)

Herod went back to the magi with good news. The king they were seeking would be born in Bethlehem, just a few miles from Jerusalem. Herod acted as excited as the magi, but with a totally different purpose. His plan was to see the child destroyed. Herod asked the magi exactly when the star had first appeared, and he asked them to let him know when they found the child so he could worship him too. What a liar—and what a coward! Herod didn't want to spark a conflict with the magi or the Parthians by telling them the truth of his intentions. He would just wait until they were headed back home to put the sword to any talk of a newborn king.

When They Saw the Star

The magi had left Herod and began to move southeast toward Bethlehem when God intervened.

The star they had seen in the east went ahead of them until it stopped over the place where the child was. When they saw the star, they were overjoyed. On coming to the house, they saw the child with his mother Mary, and they bowed down and worshiped him. Then they opened their treasures and presented him with gifts of gold and of incense and of myrrh. (Matthew 2:9-11)

If Herod was shocked to see magi in his courtyard, imagine how amazed Mary and Joseph must have been to open the door and find such startling visitors. Their humble dwelling was suddenly filled with richly dressed foreigners, bowing down in worship to a young child. I'm not sure what Mary expected to happen in the months following Jesus' dedication in the temple, but I think it's safe to say that a visit from Parthian priests was not part of her imagination.

There are three hints in this passage that the magi did not come to the stable where Jesus was born. They were not at the manger. First, in verse 11 the text says that they came to the "house" where Jesus was. The stable would have been just a cave or at best a shed. Apparently Joseph and Mary stayed in Bethlehem for a while after Jesus was born. The second clue is that Matthew repeatedly refers to Jesus as the "child." He uses the Greek word *paidion,* which was used of a child after infancy. In contrast Luke says that the shepherds found Mary and the "baby" in the manger. Luke's word is *brephos,* meaning infant or newborn. The third reason I think this was several months after Jesus' birth is that later, when Herod tried to destroy Jesus, he killed all the male children in Bethlehem under two years old. Herod had asked the magi when the star had first appeared so he could calculate about how old the child would be. Just for good measure, he had *every* boy under two years old killed.

Making It Personal

I find three significant responses to Jesus in this account. The first response was hatred and hostility. That came from Herod. Herod was afraid that this king would intrude on his life. The Messiah would change things, and Herod didn't want that. So he tried to eliminate the Son of God. Herod was more interested in saving his throne than in saving his soul.

Herod's response is still the response of a lot of people to Jesus, even a lot of "religious" people. The Jesus Seminar has received national and international media attention for their debates over what Jesus really said and did. Most of the record of the New Testament is simply written off as the additions of later writers who wanted to make Jesus out to be far more than he ever claimed to be. Any reference to his deity or lordship or unique relationship to the Father is simply penciled out of the Bible. The Jesus that is left is easy to accept. He makes no spiritual demands at all!

Maybe Herod's response is your response to Jesus. You haven't tried to kill him, but you've refused to believe in him as your Savior and Lord. You refuse to accept him because he will make some changes in your life. You have tried to explain him away, but you *know* that he is the Savior and you *know* that you need saving.

The second response to Jesus is almost worse than Herod's. The scribes and priests simply shrug their shoulders in cold indifference. These religious leaders were so engrossed in their theological debates and their lists of rules that it didn't even matter to them that Jesus was born. That's painful to think about! Some of us who are church leaders find ourselves cranking out the programs of worship with cold indifference to the very person we are seeking to please. We can tell you all the reasons why we are doctrinally correct, but we can't remember the last time we were brought low in humble confession or adoration before the One we claim to follow as Lord.

It's not just church leaders who can be afflicted with hardening of the spiritual arteries. Many Christians simply nod a little approval to Jesus by going to church on Sunday, but the rest of the time Jesus has very little part in their lives. You may be so engrossed in *your* job and *your* life and *your* work that you just ignore the lordship of Christ over your life. I remind my congregation and myself often that we don't *make* Jesus Lord of our lives. He *is* Lord! We just live like he is Lord or we live like *we* are.

The best response, of course, comes from the magi. They came into the house where Jesus and Mary lived, and they worshiped him—not *her*, Mary, or *them*, but Jesus alone. The word used in verse 11 of their worship is a word used in the New Testament to refer only to the worship of God. These magi knew that Jesus was more than a king; he was God with us. Their worship was expressed not only through adoration but also through sacrifice. They gave Jesus gifts of gold and valuable aromatic oils, gifts for a king, gifts for God.

If you have never responded to Jesus with worship, or if it's been a long time since your heart was moved to adoration or sacrifice for him, you can't do anything more appropriate than to lay this book aside and bow before him. God doesn't want great political leaders like Herod to build his kingdom. God isn't even looking for people with great knowledge, like the scribes. What God seeks first are men and women who are willing to bend their knees and bow their hearts in faith and worship to his Son.

I'm sure Mary had a response to all of this too. We have already seen that Mary was a person who treasured significant events in her heart and turned them over and over in an attempt to understand the meaning and personal implications of those events. Mary was also beginning to realize that the appearance of the angel so many months earlier had been just the first of God's surprises. Sometimes incredible blessings may come into our lives when we simply open the door to strangers.

Chapter 8

FINDING
THE PATH

A *new crisis erupted shortly after the wise men left. They were* warned in a dream not to return to Herod but to make the trip home by a different route (Matthew 2:12). Soon after, Joseph was again warned by an angel in a dream. The angel said, "Get up, take the child and his mother and escape to Egypt. Stay there until I tell you, for Herod is going to search for the child to kill him" (Matthew 2:13).

Since the message came to Joseph, Mary now not only had to trust in God but had to trust also that God was leading in her life through her husband. Joseph didn't even wait for morning light. He roused Mary, and they quickly packed their belongings and left Bethlehem.

The distance from Bethlehem to the border of Egypt was about two hundred miles through desolate, barren territory. Probably Joseph and Mary joined a caravan on its way to Egypt, since this was the best protection against robbers. Egypt, of course, was the ancient site of Israel's slavery, but since Herod's reign had begun forty years earlier Egypt had become a refuge for Jews fleeing from Herod's terror. Tradition says that the family journeyed to an area near present-day Cairo; in that area today believers can visit a church and a shrine to the holy family. The treasures given to them by the magi provided for their needs on the journey and during their stay in Egypt.

All we know for certain about the trip Joseph and Mary made to Egypt is what is recorded in Matthew 2:14. We aren't told exactly where they lived or how long they stayed or even the route they took. Several apocryphal Christian writings composed in the centuries after the completion of the New Testament try to fill in the gaps with fanciful stories about the sojourn in Egypt. They give us some insight into how quickly legends about Jesus and Mary began to emerge within the Christian community.

According to the *Arabic Gospel of the Infancy,* Joseph and Mary were attacked by two bandits on the road to Egypt, but the bandits found nothing to steal. Instead one the bandits took pity on them and gave them money; the other refused to help the poor couple. The legend goes on to say that the baby then predicted that both bandits would come in contact with him again in the future—more than thirty years in the future. They would be the two bandits crucified on either side of Jesus. The compassionate thief would repent and receive forgiveness from Jesus; the obstinate one would die condemned.[1]

Another legendary story comes from the *Gospel of Pseudo-Matthew.* Mary became hungry on the journey and looked with longing at the fruit of a date palm, hanging far above her. The infant Jesus smiled and commanded the palm to bend down so Mary could pick the dates.[2] We are told in another place in *Pseudo-Matthew* that when Mary, Joseph and the child reached their destination, Mary happened to carry Jesus into a pagan temple filled with idols. The idols all fell down before them and broke into pieces.[3] Legends about the journey into Egypt abounded in the Middle Ages. Animals are said to have bowed down in worship; Jesus' bath water cured a leper; and an exasperated Jesus turned teasing boys into goats and back into boys again.

Persecuted for Christ's Sake

Joseph and Mary stand first in a long line of people persecuted for their relationship and loyalty to Jesus. It may surprise you to know that the century marked by the most oppression against Christians is not the first or second century, when thousands died in Roman arenas. More men and women and families have suffered and died for Christ in the twentieth century than in all other centuries combined, and the twenty-first doesn't promise much improvement. Christians in every part of the world have witnessed persecution and upheaval.

The Boxer uprising in China set the tone for the twentieth century. In the year 1900, 135 missionaries and 53 children were killed by bare-chested supporters of the Chinese emperor. Hundreds of Chinese Christians lost their lives or went into hiding. But the church was not crushed. The courage of those martyrs spurred revival in the years that followed. By 1911 most political leaders in the Republic of China professed to be Christians. In Nazi Germany and Communist Russia, tens of thousands of Christians were imprisoned, tortured and killed. Africa exploded in the 1960s against any Western presence, including missionaries and African converts to Christianity. Even today Christian people in southern Sudan are under fierce attack from Muslims in the northern part of the country. Whole villages of people are slaughtered, and the children disappear into a slave market that thrives across northern Africa.[4]

I remember not many years ago saying goodby to a young man leaving our church to return to Pakistan. He had come to the United States for his education and now was returning home to take a prominent place in government service. While in America, he had heard the gospel and believed on Jesus Christ as Savior and Lord. Now he had to go back to a land where conversion from Islam was punishable by death. I've often wondered what became of him.

Those of us living in the United States or other democratic nations may yet see oppression or persecution. As our culture becomes more secular and more willing to compromise moral standards, the conscience-prodding voice of committed Christians will be less tolerated. We shouldn't be surprised by that trend. Jesus said that the world would hate us just like it hated him (John 15:18-19). What we can expect from an unbelieving world, cut loose from the moral constraints of biblical truth, is not acceptance or tolerance but tribulation (John 16:33).

Rachel Weeping for Her Children

Herod's reaction to the magi's failure to return to him with any information about the child was swift and brutal. He ordered his soldiers to slaughter all male children two years old and younger in the town of Bethlehem and in the rural areas around it. Some critics of the Bible have put a big question mark over the story of Herod's slaughter of the children. They believe that the brutality of the event makes it historically suspect, especially since there are no references to this incident in any sources outside the New Testament. The atrocity seems so horrible that it could not escape the notice of first-century writers.

Several factors, however, need to be considered. First, in spite of the human suffering involved, this took place in a relatively insignificant area of Palestine, which was itself on the frontier of the empire, far removed from Rome. The world of New

Testament Palestine was a world filled with brutality and acts of human cruelty. In comparison with other events this slaughter fades in significance. The town of Bethlehem was small. Estimates of the number of children killed by Herod's soldiers range as high as three hundred, but most scholars place the number at about twenty. Overshadowing all other factors was the cruelty of Herod the Great. He was infamous for his inhumanity. He ordered the murder of his own wife, Mariamne, and three of his sons. Several times in his reign he had ordered mass executions and crucifixions. He would not have hesitated for a moment to destroy a few young children if it would have rid him of a potential rival to his throne and power. Few ancient rulers could rival Herod for his savagery.

Augustus, the Roman emperor, would probably not have interfered in this matter, since the Romans considered the Jews the most difficult of their subjects to rule. Furthermore, Augustus had given his permission for the murder of Herod's sons and had not been beyond using murder and massacre in his own rise to political power. As cruel and brutal as the story reads to us today, there is no reason to doubt its truthfulness. In fact, it confirms everything we know about Herod and his oppressive rule.

Matthew, the only Gospel writer to relate the story of Herod's slaughter of the children, saw something beyond the bare facts of the king's rage and Joseph's dream. He saw God using the choices and actions of human beings to fulfill prophecies spoken hundreds of years earlier. In their original context, some of these prophecies had nothing directly to do with the coming Messiah. But as Matthew looked back at the Old Testament with Spirit-filled eyes, he saw the hints of these events glinting in the sand of the ancient records. God called Israel out of Egypt in the exodus under Moses, and now he calls his own Son from the same land (Matthew 2:15; Hosea 11:1).

The sound of women's weeping that rose from the homes of Bethlehem after Herod's slaughter was the same lament ("Rachel's weeping") that arose six hundred years earlier in Ramah as Jews were rounded up there to be taken away into captivity in Babylon (Matthew 2:18; Jeremiah 31:15; 40:1).

The Tyrant Dies

Historians are able to pinpoint the date of Herod's death pretty accurately at 4 B.C. Jesus, obviously, was born several months before Herod's death. Most New Testament scholars date Jesus' birth at 6-5 B.C. It seems a little strange to have Jesus born "before Christ" (B.C.), but the problem came hundreds of years later when the Western calendar was converted from a Roman time frame to a Christian one.[5]

When Herod died, the angel appeared again to Joseph just as he had promised and told him that it was safe to return to Jewish territory. Mary, Joseph and the baby again made the long journey across the northern Sinai to Judea. Their first plan, apparently, was to return to Bethlehem in Judea, but as they approached the border they heard some disturbing news.

After Herod died, the Jewish people pleaded with the Roman emperor to return their land to religious rule under a Jewish governor. Herod had claimed to be Jewish in his faith, but he was an Edomite (or Idumean) by birth. Furthermore, his appointment as king of the Jews had wiped out the last remnants of Jewish self-rule that remained from the glorious days of the Maccabees more than a hundred years earlier. The emperor, however, decided to divide Herod's kingdom among Herod's sons.

Judea, Samaria and Herod's homeland of Idumea were given to Archelaus. He possessed all of his father's bad traits and none of his father's abilities. Archelaus began his reign by slaughtering three thousand Jews in the temple who had decided to raise a rebellion against him. News like that prompted Joseph and Mary to make another change in direction. They decided to return to Nazareth in Galilee. Archelaus ruled only about ten years (until A.D. 6). Jewish protests became so vehement that he was deposed and replaced by Roman governors, the most notable of whom was Pontius Pilate, who ruled from A.D. 26 to 36.

Another son, probably the most capable of Herod's boys, had been made tetrarch of Galilee and Perea. Herod Antipas ruled there forty years. He would foolishly order the execution of John the Baptist (Mark 6:17-28) and ridicule Jesus before his crucifixion (Luke 23:6-12), but overall he was the mildest of the Herodian rulers. Back in Nazareth, Joseph, Mary and Jesus again settled down to the quiet life of a small village.

Making It Personal

I'm struck as I read this account of the escape to Egypt that God did not miraculously deliver Joseph and Mary or even Jesus from harm or struggle or difficulty. Despite later legends of miraculous help for the family on the way to Egypt, Matthew gives us no indication of bending palm trees or generous bandits. Mary and Joseph had to run for their lives. The difficulty of travel with a young child was no different for them from what it was for any other couple back then, or today. The pictures flashed across our television screens of refugees on the run from war or massacre could very well reflect the fear and exhaustion and terror that filled the faces of Mary and Joseph. The birth in a stable and the flight to Egypt were just the first steps in the process for Jesus. Even as a baby he was learning maturity by the things he experienced (Hebrews 5:8-9). He was identifying with the trials of those he came to redeem.

I don't know about you, but I find it difficult to trust God's leading sometimes, especially in times of upheaval or dramatic change. If I had been in Joseph's place, I might have stayed in Bethlehem a little longer just to pray about such a drastic move. I would have at least waited for daylight! Joseph and Mary, however, were willing to trust God even when they didn't see how everything would work out.

Several years ago, at a time of pain and tremendous difficulty in our lives, we were left with no option, it seemed, except to move our family to our home town and into my parents' house. Since my parents were overseas for a year, their home was available, but it had only one bedroom, and we had two teenagers and a baby on the way. We had prayed for God's leading; we just couldn't believe he was leading us to this place at this time. I can still remember the sinking feeling in my heart and the gnawing confusion in my mind as we unloaded our clothes and moved into that tiny house. Many months passed before we could look back and see God's hand in this event. If you had asked us at the time if we were in God's will, we would have said, "We just don't know." But as we took one step at a time and held on to him through tears and confusion, we found ourselves led into whole new areas of ministry and relationships.

Mary and Joseph learned through trial and testing to trust God. That's how we learn to trust him too. They had an angel's voice to guide them; we have someone far greater. We are led by the Spirit, God himself, who dwells within us as believers. Even in the darkest night, even through the most difficult transitions, we can be confident of his direction, wisdom and love.

Chapter 9

RAISING GOD'S SON

*M*y wife, Karen, and I have started over as parents. We had two children in our twenties and enjoyed watching them grow up into young adulthood. But as we approached forty, we found out another child was on the way. Kyle is a joy to be around, and he is keeping us young! We get to go back to elementary school and help with class parties and sit through Christmas concerts.

The one great fear I have had since Kyle was born is that somehow he will be taken from us—snatched, kidnapped, stolen. It's an irrational fear. We've never had a child get lost and we've never been threatened, but the fear is still there. Usually it just sits in a dark corner of my mind like a rat gnawing away in a damp cellar. Occasionally it rises up with incredible power. Karen has talked me through it several times. I have prayed about it repeatedly, but it still lingers. Every time it clouds my spirit and chokes my emotions I am forced to give my fear—and my son—over to the care and concern of my Father.

I wonder if what I feel at times is the same panic that gripped Mary and Joseph when they looked for Jesus one evening among their relatives and friends and couldn't find him. They had all traveled together from Nazareth in Galilee to Jerusalem in Judea for the festival of Passover. After the pageantry of the temple sacrifice and the Passover feast with family members, Mary and Joseph had packed their belongings and started back home. Jesus wasn't in their sight, but they assumed that he was with the other boys. It was only when they had set up camp for the night and began to ask around that they discovered Jesus was missing.

Growing Up in Nazareth

The Bible doesn't tell us much about the years of Jesus' childhood and young adulthood. But, as happens so often, when Scripture is silent, folklore tries to fill that tantalizing gap in the story. The *Infancy Gospel of Thomas* focuses almost entirely on the "hidden years" of Jesus in Nazareth. One story this apocryphal gospel tells takes place when Jesus is five years old. He is playing near a pool and makes twelve sparrows out of soft clay. When someone complains to Joseph that Jesus is profaning the sabbath day by making such objects, Jesus claps his hands, and the birds come to life and fly away. Other stories picture Jesus raising a boy back to life who had fallen from a rooftop and healing a man who had injured his foot with an ax.

Not all the stories are positive, however. In some of the accounts Jesus is little more than a spoiled brat. He curses a child who muddies the pool of water Jesus is playing in; he gets angry with a boy who bumps against him and the boy falls down dead. Adults who try to rebuke Jesus are stricken with blindness. Even Joseph is threatened by Jesus when Joseph pulls Jesus by the ear in discipline.[1]

In contrast to the fanciful stories that emerged in later centuries, Luke summarizes the first twelve years of Jesus' childhood with a few simple words: "And the child grew and became strong; he was filled with wisdom, and the grace of God was upon him" (Luke 2:40). While we would certainly like more details, Luke's statement conveys quite a bit about Jesus' early years. It tells us that Jesus grew up pretty much like every other child in Nazareth. So what we know about Jewish culture in the first century gives us some insight into the home life of Mary and Joseph and their son Jesus.

When Joseph and Mary returned to Nazareth after their stay in Egypt, life took on a sense of normal routine. Joseph went back to his work as a carpenter; Mary worked in their home and nurtured her son. Luke's comment that Jesus "grew and became strong" lets us know that Jesus grew from infancy to childhood just like every other child. In the Jewish society of that day, the parents took the responsibility for the early religious training and education of their children. Jesus would have learned to speak Aramaic, the language of the Jews. He would have been told the great stories of his people—the escape from Pharaoh, the majesty of King David, the faithfulness of Daniel. Simple songs of praise, the basic creeds of the faith and child-level prayers began to spring from Jesus' lips as his parents guided him in the first steps of obedience.

At the age of five or six Jesus would have attended the synagogue school to learn to read the Scriptures in Hebrew and to write the letters of the sacred text. Reading and writing were important tools to every Jewish boy and girl because the Jews were people of the Book, the Torah, God's Word.

It's not easy for us as Christians to think about Jesus as a "normal" boy learning his alphabet in school. We have been so impressed with Jesus' deity that we forget to balance his deity with his humanity. Jesus was not God pretending to be a human being; he was God who had become fully human. That means Jesus had to learn to crawl and walk and read. He was a sinless human being, so he never committed moral error, but our view of Jesus' sinlessness does not mean that he couldn't make a mistake in multiplication as he learned the basics of arithmetic. Just as Jesus grew and developed physically, he grew and developed intellectually—and Jesus apparently was an excellent student. He immersed himself in the Scriptures and drank deeply at the well of biblical truth. In the later years of his ministry Jesus quoted from every section of the Bible with ease and accuracy. He memorized key passages and meditated quietly about the significance and meaning of the Law and the Prophets.

Jesus learned the rituals of the faith too—the weekly sabbath, the annual cycle of feasts and fasting, the importance of sacrifice. The obedience to the Law of Moses that Jesus saw modeled in Joseph and Mary was not dead, rigid legalism. Joseph and Mary knew the delight and joy of faith in God, and they kept the requirements of the Law with hearts of gratitude and love. Devotion to the Lord was not something peripheral to their lives; it was central. Decisions about work, family, leisure, finances, commitments of time and energy were made in full, conscious surrender to the rule of God over their lives as King.

About My Father's Business

It was this focused obedience to the Lord that brought Mary and Joseph and Jesus to Jerusalem in Jesus' twelfth year. They came for the celebration of the Passover, the joyous reminder of Israel's escape from slavery in Egypt. Fifteen hundred years had passed since God had set his people free, but the memory of God's incredible deliverance had not faded. Jesus may have come every year to Jerusalem with his parents, but it was particularly important that he came as a twelve-year-old. The Jews believed that at the age of thirteen a boy took upon himself the responsibility of obedience to the Law. The concept developed much later in Judaism into the ceremony of the *bar mitzvah* ("son of the covenant"). In preparation for that important spiritual transition, Jesus traveled with his parents to Jerusalem to celebrate the feast.

Their journey came at a particularly troubled time in Judea. Herod's son Archelaus had ruled so poorly that his subjects had sent a delegation of protest to the emperor. After hearing their complaint, Augustus banished Archelaus to Gaul (modern France) and instituted direct Roman rule over Judea through a Roman governor. The Jews were pleased that Archelaus had been removed, but they were distressed by what they saw as even more direct oppression by Roman authority. A revolt was sparked by Judas of Galilee. The revolt was suppressed in A.D. 7, but tensions in Jerusalem were high, especially during the feasts. The potential for violence hung over the city like a dark, threatening cloud.

When Mary and Joseph discovered that Jesus was missing from the group returning to Nazareth, they had every reason to be concerned. It was not a good time for a young boy to be missing. They spent that night in anxious concern and, at first light, headed back to Jerusalem. By the time they had traveled one day's journey away from Jerusalem and one day's journey back and then began to search the next morning, Jesus had been missing almost three days.

Jesus was perfectly safe the whole time. He had gone into the temple complex and had stayed there. As the religious teachers gathered to discuss the Law, Jesus sat with the other students. At first Jesus listened with deep interest. Then he asked a question, as rabbis in training had a right to do. The question astonished the teachers almost as much as the source of the question. This twelve-year-old boy had a profound grasp of biblical truth. His question pierced to the heart of their discussion. Thoughtfully the religious scholars replied, and their reply prompted another question, equally perceptive and penetrating. Everyone who heard Jesus was amazed at the question he asked and at the level of spiritual understanding he revealed.

One common misconception about this incident is that Jesus was *teaching* the religious leaders of Israel. Luke makes it clear that Jesus was listening to the teachers and asking them questions (Luke 2:46). In this setting Jesus was the learner, not the teacher. But his questions displayed a depth of knowledge and maturity that few adults had reached, much less a twelve-year-old. This is the only time in the Gospels where Jesus is pictured as learning from the religious leaders of Israel. In the later years of his ministry Jesus would expose most of the teaching of the scribes and scholars as empty words produced by men whose hearts were far from God.

A Worried Mother

Joseph and Mary were just as astonished as everyone else when they saw what was going on. But it was Mary who took the initiative in rebuking Jesus. "Son," she said, "why have you treated us like this? Your father and I have been anxiously searching for you" (Luke 2:48).

On the Fourth of July a few years ago, our family went with some friends to the Civil War battlefield at Antietam. Twenty-five thousand people spread blankets and picnic suppers over a grassy slope as we waited for a concert and a fireworks display. Our son Kevin, a young teenager, decided to do a little exploring in the concession area. After an hour I went looking for him. When I came back to the group without him, we all got a little nervous. As we scanned the enormous crowd, one of our friends pointed and said, "Isn't that Kevin?" He had spotted Kevin about two hundred yards away!

I picked my way across the hillside and came up behind Kevin, who by this time was frantic himself. All I said was his name. He wheeled around to me, and the tough-guy façade of a young teenager dissolved into tears. We stood there awhile until the tears were over and then made our way back to everyone else.

Later that night my relief at finding him gave way to a little parental rebuke. "We were worried, Kevin. Don't ever wander off in a place like that until you take your bearings and know how to get back. Didn't you think about telling a security officer that you were lost?"

I felt that day a little of what Mary felt! Here was Jesus, their obedient, studious son, doing something totally out of character. At least it seemed that way to her. She was relieved to find him but was also wounded by his apparent disregard for her feelings and her worry as a mother. "Why have you treated us this way?"

When I attended seminary in Winona Lake, Indiana, the summer Bible conferences in the huge, old Billy Sunday Tabernacle were still being held. I would try to slip into the meetings whenever I got a chance. I remember hearing a sermon one warm summer evening based on this account of Jesus in the temple. The Bible teacher had some pretty harsh words for Mary. He felt that she should have known that Jesus was in the temple. He also thought Mary and Joseph should have taken a seat and waited until Jesus was ready to leave. After all, he reasoned, hadn't Mary been told by Gabriel and by old Simeon that Jesus was the Messiah? Didn't she realize that she was rebuking the Son of God?

I had a real problem that night with his evaluation of Mary, and that was before I had any kids of my own. Twelve years in Mary's life had intervened since the angel's visit and Simeon's prophecy. In those twelve years Jesus had seemed pretty normal, more sensitive than most boys, certainly more obedient and trustworthy than any child, but otherwise normal. Now Jesus stays behind in Jerusalem, knowing his parents are headed home. He's not worried, wondering if they will come back for him; he's in the temple asking questions. If I had been Mary I would have been more than a little upset!

Jesus' response is not a "slap in the face" (as the preacher I heard put it). Jesus expresses his own surprise at Mary's concern. Jesus thought they would know where to look for him. "Why were you searching for me?" he asked. "Didn't you know I had to be in my Father's house?" (Luke 2:49). The phrase "in my Father's house" is tricky to translate. Jesus could mean several related things: "Didn't you know I had to be among my Father's things, about my Father's business, involved with issues related to my Father?"

From our perspective on this side of the cross and with plenty of hindsight to help, we understand what Jesus meant. He had come to the full awareness of who he was—Joseph's "son" in one sense but God's "Son" in a far more important sense. Mary was concerned that Jesus had worried his adopted father; Jesus was intent on pleasing his heavenly Father.

These are the earliest actual words of Jesus recorded anywhere in the Gospels. Jesus is not spoken to or about but finds his own voice. Apart from the events surrounding Jesus' birth, Luke is the only Gospel writer to tell us anything about the first thirty years of Jesus' life. He includes this incident to show us that by the age of twelve, Jesus knew he was the Messiah, the unique Son of God. If you are thinking, *But Jesus knew who he was all along,* you are forgetting that Jesus became fully human. In the words of the apostle Paul, Jesus "emptied himself"

(Philippians 2:6-7 NASB)—not of deity but of the use of his attributes of deity. Jesus did not live his life as God pretending to be a human being but as a fully Spirit-controlled man. Just as Jesus had to learn to speak and write, he had to come to his own self-awareness. Jesus had to reach his own personal understanding that he was God's Anointed One.

A number of factors led Jesus to that conclusion. Undoubtedly Mary and Joseph had told Jesus the story of his miraculous conception. The words of the angel, the visit of the magi, the clear divine protection over his early life would have made a profound impression on him. Probably the most powerful source of his self-recognition came from the Scriptures. As Jesus read the words of the Hebrew Bible, he began to see himself. The Spirit of God who dwelt intimately and powerfully in Jesus brought assurance to his young heart that he was, in fact, the promised Messiah, God in the flesh.

We have the biblical and historical perspective to understand Jesus' words to his mother, but Mary must have been perplexed. *She* knows who Jesus is, but she is suddenly jolted by the fact that *Jesus* now knows fully who he is. Luke is quick to add that Mary and Joseph "did not understand" what Jesus was saying (Luke 2:50). The full impact of Jesus' claim that God was his Father in a unique way came only as they had time to quietly reflect on what Jesus had said.

The curtain drops on this scene in the temple, and eighteen more years of Jesus' life pass in silence. This would not be the last time that Mary and Joseph had to fine-tune their minds and attitudes toward their son. They had a young man focused on his own destiny—a destiny that would change the human condition forever. But Jesus would not become a rebel in his home or a mystic sitting in a cave. Jesus demonstrated his submission to his heavenly Father by living in submission to his earthly parents. "Then he went down to Nazareth with them and was obedient to them. But his mother treasured all these things in her heart. And Jesus grew in wisdom and stature, and in favor with God and men" (Luke 2:51-52).

I'm sure that the people of Nazareth looked on young Jesus as a nice boy, even as an extraordinary student, but in the end they were convinced that he was pretty much like they were. In the years of his ministry Jesus came to Nazareth often and even worshiped in the synagogue there. On one occasion Jesus read a prophecy about the Messiah from Isaiah's book and then announced: "Today this scripture is fulfilled in your hearing!" (Luke 4:21). His own friends and old school chums took offense at Jesus. They were so furious that this hometown boy would claim to be the Anointed One that they tried to push him off a cliff to his death (Luke 4:29-30).

Making It Personal

I wish we knew more about Jesus' young years. How did his parents deal with a perfect son? What did Jesus do to prepare himself for the intensity of the three years of his public ministry? I find myself asking out of my own curiosity what the people of Nazareth asked out of unbelief: "Where did this man get his wisdom?" Jesus' character was certainly molded by the Scriptures and by God's Spirit, but it was also marked by Joseph and Mary. Neither one of them was a great scholar or preacher. They lived fairly routine lives. But in the ordinary events of life Joseph and Mary modeled a consistent pattern of faithfulness and obedience and love for God.

I sometimes think that the big dramatic things make the greatest impression on my children—taking my son to a Promise Keepers rally, being asked to speak to a large audience at a Bible conference, planning that great family vacation, receiving recognition from people around me. Mary and Joseph have convinced me that we make our most indelible impressions on our children in the quiet, mundane routine of life. I wonder how much love for God and faithful obedience to his Word my family sees as we sit down for a meal, as we rake leaves in the yard, as I drive them to school, as I tuck them in at night. Over the long haul, the words I speak on Sundays will probably mean very little. What those around me, especially my kids, will follow is what they see in me the rest of the week.

Chapter 10

A LIFE
IN THE SHADOWS

*M*ary *was the kind of mother you want to live near. I've*
known people who have moved several states or several time
zones away from home just to escape overbearing, obsessive
parents. But Mary wasn't like that.

When Jesus was about thirty years old, his three years of
public ministry began. But Jesus didn't just wake up one
morning, pack his bags and leave home. The first year of his
ministry was a year of transition. Jesus was baptized in the
Jordan River by his relative John and then spent six weeks in
the wilderness, enduring the temptations of Satan. After that
Jesus spent a lot of time at home.

John is the only Gospel writer to tell us much about the first
year of Jesus' work, a year of relative obscurity. The other
Gospels begin their story with Jesus calling Peter, Andrew,
James and John to follow him as disciples. I was always confused

by those stories when I heard them in Sunday school. I imagined Peter and Andrew mending their nets on the shore of the Sea of Galilee, whistling the latest "hits," minding their own business. Suddenly, an unknown man came up to them and said, "Follow me!" and, almost as if they were hypnotized, the four fishermen dropped everything and followed Jesus.

In John's Gospel, however, we find that Jesus met these men on several occasions before he called them to follow him. They spent time together but not yet on a permanent basis. Jesus was developing a relationship with these men, and they were beginning to recognize the spiritual greatness of Jesus. They knew that in time the call to follow Jesus permanently would come, and they had already decided that when the call came they would follow.

It is during that first year of transition ministry that we find Jesus and Mary together at a celebration. "A wedding took place at Cana in Galilee. Jesus' mother was there, and Jesus and his disciples [only four or five men at this point] had also been invited to the wedding" (John 2:1-2). Cana was just a few miles from Jesus' hometown. It's possible that this was the wedding of one of Jesus' relatives and that Mary was acting as the hostess. She seems to be responsible to see that everything went smoothly.

Overseeing a wedding is a difficult job anytime, but it was especially stressful in Jesus' day. Today we come to a church, witness the ceremony, go to the reception for a few hours and then go home. All that's left for the family to do is clean up and pay the bills! In Jesus' day, the parents of the bride and groom got things started years earlier. They made a contract for the marriage when their children were very young. My occasional threats to pick mates for my own children are always met with smiles and rolled eyes and that particularly exasperated look from my wife, but in the first century that was how it was done.

When the wedding day came, the groom with all the guests made a long, noisy procession to the bride's house. The wedding vows were spoken at the bride's home. Then the groom took the bride by the hand, and the procession went back to the groom's home or to his parents' home. A jubilant feast followed. The wedding feast lasted from two to seven days—a reception for a week!

The groom's parents were responsible to feed and care for all the guests the whole time. If they ran out of food or wine during the feast, it was considered an insult to the guests and a humiliation for the family. Not having enough to eat and drink was the one thing you never wanted to happen, but on this occasion it did. The wine was gone (John 2:3).

Since we never read of Joseph in this passage, most Bible scholars conclude that Joseph had died sometime in Jesus' early adulthood.[1] As the oldest son of the family, Jesus now had the responsibility of caring for Mary and helping her. So when this problem came up, she went to Jesus for help. I don't think Mary had any idea about what Jesus would do, but she knew he would help her somehow.[2]

Talking to Your Mother

Nowhere in the New Testament is Jesus said to call Mary "mother." In fact his reply to her here seems disrespectful. "Woman, what do I have to do with you?" (John 2:4 NASB). The Greek text is even more curt: "What is this of yours to me?" or "How does this problem of yours involve me?"

When Jesus calls Mary "woman," it is not a sign of disrespect; the title is actually a very tender form of reference. He uses the same word to address his mother when he is dying on the cross. The New International Version comes closer to the meaning with "dear woman." "Dear woman," Jesus says, "how does this problem of wine involve me?" Then he adds, "My time has not yet come." Repeatedly in John's Gospel Jesus talks about "my time" or "my hour," referring to the time of his death. What he means here is that the focus of his life is on his ultimate destiny, not on following instructions from his mother. Mary may have implied some command or demand in her statement to Jesus, such as "They have no wine. Go get some."

Jesus, however, has reached maturity. His ministry had started, and he's already begun to gather disciples. Jesus had fully made the transition that began eighteen years earlier in the temple. His focus is on the ultimate purpose of his life. Mary has not yet made the transition from parent to follower. Jesus is no longer under her authority; he is under the Father's authority. When the Father says, "This is your time," Jesus will obey. His words were a gentle but needed rebuke to Mary.

Mary understood Jesus' words, at least in part. She turned and walked away with one simple command to the servants: "Do whatever he tells you" (John 2:5). Within minutes Jesus miraculously made more than one hundred gallons of water into fine wine. Jesus did not do the miracle simply to save a bridegroom from embarrassment; he did it to reveal his own glory (John 2:11). Jesus was not responding to Mary's direction but to his Father's will. Somehow the Father prompted Jesus to perform the first of thousands of mighty works of power.

The disciples responded exactly the way they should have responded to a wondrous work of God, by putting their faith in Jesus. They were already persuaded that Jesus had great spiritual insight and a godly character. Now they came to realize that Jesus was the promised Messiah. The ancient prophets had said repeatedly that the coming of the Anointed One would be marked by an abundance of miraculous deeds.[3] What the disciples saw at the wedding in Cana moved their relationship with Jesus to a whole new level.

Mary's Message

When I began to think about Mary as a model for spiritual growth, I also began to watch the bookstore shelves for books about Mary. In the last few years the religion section at our local mall bookstore has featured several books about Mary and her reported appearances. One book that caught my eye a few months ago was titled *Mary's Final Message to the World*. The author takes all the statements from people who claim to have received some message from Mary and tries to distill everything down to a few basic directives from Mary to the world.

Mary's statement to the servants at the wedding in Cana are the last direct words of Mary recorded in the Bible. Mary appears several more times in the biblical record, but none of her statements is recorded. It's almost as if the Spirit of God, as he directed the writing of Scripture, wanted to preserve the profound impact of these words from Mary: "Do whatever he tells you."

I certainly don't want to spiritualize Mary's statement beyond the context of John 2, but it seems to me that this is a more reliable message to us than anything received through those who claim to have seen or heard Mary in the last two thousand years. "Do whatever *he* tells you to do." Mary points away from herself as the solution to the problem and points to her son alone.

Seen in that light, Mary's words have profound implications in some important areas of Christian thought and practice. In worship, for example, our praise and adoration are to be directed to Christ, not to Mary. The Roman Catholic Church makes an official distinction between *adoration* (which belongs to God alone) and *veneration* (a lesser form of devotion directed to Mary, the saints and even angels).[4] While Catholic theology makes that official distinction, in Catholic practice it seems difficult to see much actual difference. The focus on

Mary in the liturgy of the church and in the beliefs of some Catholics elevates her to a level virtually equal with Christ. Pope John Paul II has been unwavering in his devotion to Mary and calls her "the Mother of God, the Mother of the Church, and our Mother in the order of grace."[5] These titles raise Mary far above any statements made about her in Scripture. The writers of the New Testament and the apostle Paul in particular were very emphatic that "in *everything*" Jesus Christ was to "have the supremacy" (Colossians 1:18). Mary is never the focus of worship in the New Testament.

No one in the New Testament ever prays to Mary, or through Mary either. Despite a long tradition of prayers addressed to Mary and hymns of exaltation to her in both the Catholic and Orthodox Churches, no hint of such a practice appears anywhere in Scripture. I understand in a sense why it seems appealing to pray to Mary. Mary seems more like we are, more approachable. If Mary stands close to Jesus (as some churches teach), why not approach her or another saint and ask them to make an appeal to Jesus or to God the Father on your behalf?

Approaching Mary in prayer may seem easier than approaching God directly, but it raises a whole host of issues from a biblical perspective. I've already pointed out one problem—we can find no hint of prayer to a saint anywhere in the Bible. Those churches that advocate praying to God through Mary or through other saints base the practice on the teaching authority of the church, not directly on any biblical example or teaching. Prayer in the New Testament is always addressed to God alone. Any member of the Trinity may be addressed in prayer, but the pattern seen most often in Scripture is to pray *to* the Father *through* the Son *by* (or *in*) the Spirit. Normally we voice our praise and requests to God the Father, the source of all good gifts (James 1:17; see also Ephesians 3:14-16). We come to the Father because Jesus, God the Son, has pioneered the way for us into the Father's presence (Hebrews 9:24; 10:21-22). Empowerment for prayer comes from the Spirit of God, who dwells in us and who moves our hearts to adoration (Ephesians 6:18). In the Bible saving grace and sustaining grace come from God alone. No apostle, no prophet, no man or woman of God is ever portrayed as a channel of grace.

It also seems to me that if we pray to Mary or pray to God through Mary, we cloud the ministry of Jesus as our priest before the Father. Jesus made the full and final sacrifice for sin, and by virtue of that sacrifice he entered into God's presence for us. He is the only mediator between God and human beings (1 Timothy 2:5). He is the only one who can put his hand on both humanity and God and who can bring peace between us. Jesus is our advocate, our priest, with the Father.

Prayer through Mary (or any saint) also clouds the biblical truth that we as believers are priests before God (Hebrews 13:15-16; 1 Peter 2:5; Revelation 1:6). When you trusted Christ as Savior and Lord, one of the blessings God gave you was to make you a priest. Every believer has the high calling of the priesthood! As priests we can come directly to God. I don't have to be so afraid of God that I stand far away from him. I don't have to ask Mary or a saint in heaven or a pastor here on earth to take my request to God because God is too busy to notice me. In the Father's presence stands my Savior, and because he is there, I can come to the Father without fear. I come with awe, I come with deep reverence for God's majesty, but I come boldly, knowing that my small concerns are, in fact, God's personal concerns (1 Peter 5:7).

Making It Personal

I had a call last week from a woman who wanted me to pray for her dissolving marriage and for her wandering husband. "Maybe if *you* pray," she said, "it will do some good. I've prayed and prayed, but nothing has changed. Maybe God will respond if you pray." I promised her I would pray, but I couldn't let her go without adding some words of instruction. I told her that God *did* hear her prayers. She had God's attention as much as I did. Enlisting other believers to pray with us is a solidly biblical practice, but we should never think that one believer's prayer goes higher or reaches closer to God than another believer's prayer.

The woman's response to what I said exposed a deeper issue than a simple misunderstanding of the theology of prayer. She said, "But I feel so unworthy. I don't feel like I can ask God for anything." That's really the problem in prayer, isn't it? How can we dare to walk into the presence of God with our seemingly puny needs? And why would the awesome, holy God reigning way up there ever be moved to consider a request from someone as unworthy of his attention as I am?

By ourselves, we *are* unworthy. In our own ragged garments, it *is* the height of presumption to address the God of eternity. But as believers we come before him clothed in the perfection of his own Son. Our sin has been removed by the sacrifice of the cross. When we received God's grace in Jesus Christ, all of Christ's righteous purity was poured out on us. We *are* sinners; we *are* unworthy of the abundance of God's blessings. But what God declares to be true is true, even if we don't always feel it's true of us.

So when I'm at the bottom, sitting in a pigpen of my own rebellious disobedience or crying in some dark emotional cave, my heavenly Father strains to hear the weakest sobs of repentance or pain. He has *made* us worthy of his attention in Christ. We are his own dear children.

Those who claim to hear Mary speak or who wait for some glimpse of her in a window or in a formation of clouds are looking in vain for some connection, some message that will bring a glimmer of hope into their lives. Mary's words in John 2 still ring powerfully today: "Do whatever he tells you to do." The focus of Mary's life, the power of Mary's testimony cuts like a laser beam to her son Jesus Christ.

Chapter 11

WHEN ANSWERS DON'T COME

Mothers have a way of knowing things about us that no one else can figure out. Several years ago I took my parents to the airport for an overseas flight that would take them away from me for a year. My own heart was a war zone. I was wrestling with the ultimate outcome of some very bad decisions I had made in my life, but only God and I knew the full story. My mother told me later that she knew I was struggling. She knew from the way I hugged her and from the way I cried that something was terribly wrong.

Mary must have struggled as she watched Jesus at the height of his ministry in Galilee. Throngs of people were coming to her son, listening to him teach, reaching out to him for healing or deliverance. He worked constantly; the crowds were always there. His disciples could sneak away and grab a quick meal or a few hours rest, but not Jesus. Everyone wanted to see him;

everyone had a need that only he could meet. People sat for hours, captivated by his words. The sick, lame, blind and deaf stood or were carried in long lines, waiting breathlessly for a touch from the miracle-worker. No one was ever turned aside; no one ever went away unchanged.

Another concern for Mary stood at the edge of the crowd. At first, only a few religious leaders watched Jesus, but every day there were more. Most of them were local rabbis, but some came from Jerusalem. They came to watch and to listen and to find fault. Their dark glances and whispered complaints were getting louder and more obvious. It would have been bad enough if Jesus had just ignored them, but he became more and more direct in his challenges to them. The Pharisees especially seemed to be the targets of his barbed rebukes. The Pharisees were returning his comments in kind, calling Jesus a drunkard and a friend to sinners and a companion of whores.

Mary had also been hearing the talk around the table at home when Jesus' brothers and sisters gathered for family meals. None of them was a follower of Jesus. They just saw him as the older brother—the one everybody (including their mother) always compared them to. Jesus had been the perfect son, always interested in the Law of Moses, always attentive to Joseph's instruction, the one who never created any trouble. Now people were beginning to call him the Messiah, the Deliverer, a prophet, a rabbi, the Christ.

His brothers thought Jesus was on the verge of a nervous breakdown or insanity (Mark 3:21). What Jesus needed was an intervention. Several family members needed to sit down and confront him with his strange behavior, his poor eating habits, his lack of concern for his own relatives and their needs. After all, since Joseph's death, the responsibility for the family's financial security fell to the oldest son, and Jesus hadn't contributed to the family coffer for months. Who better to lead the charge, to penetrate Jesus' overworked brain, than his own mother? Perhaps out of genuine concern, perhaps caving in to family pressure, Mary accompanied Jesus' brothers as they made their way to the house where Jesus was preaching.

Are Not His Brothers Among Us?

A lot of controversy has centered around the brothers and sisters of Jesus. Who exactly were they? Several references are made to them in the New Testament,[1] and in two passages his brothers are named. When Jesus came to Nazareth, for example, and began to teach in his hometown synagogue, the people responded with amazement.

"Where did this man get these things?" they asked. "What's this wisdom that has been given him, that he even does miracles! Isn't this the carpenter? Isn't this Mary's son and the brother of James, Joseph, Judas and Simon? Aren't his sisters here with us?" And they took offense at him. (Mark 6:2-3; see also Matthew 13:54-56)

The normal reading of that passage leads us to believe that Jesus grew up in a family with four younger brothers and at least two sisters.[2] Actually, they were half-siblings since they had the same mother but Joseph was not Jesus' biological father. In other words, after Jesus' miraculous conception and birth, Mary and Joseph entered into a normal marriage relationship from which six or more other children were born. But that is just one interpretation. Some Christians read these verses very differently.

Epiphanius, a church father living in the fourth century, argued that these were sons and daughters of Joseph by a previous marriage. According to this view, Joseph was a widower when he married Mary, and he brought these children with him into the marriage. Jerome, who also lived in the fourth century, claimed that these six people were not true brothers and sisters at all. They were cousins or other relatives. He understood the terms *brothers* and *sisters* to refer in a looser sense to any relative.[3]

Both Jerome and Epiphanius came up with their views in order to defend the emerging belief of the church in the perpetual virginity of Mary. At this point in church history, Mary was beginning to be exalted by church theologians. The virgin conception of Jesus had been affirmed as true doctrine since the beginning of the church, but now theologians thought they had to extend the barrier of virginity beyond the conception and birth of Jesus. The church's teaching on the perpetual virginity of Mary simply said that Mary never had a sexual encounter with a man ever.[4] Joseph married her at the Lord's command but never had sexual contact with her. The birth of six children, of course, would require sexual contact, so the church leaders began to search for another explanation for the brothers and sisters of Jesus.

The third and fourth centuries of the church also saw a tremendous upsurge of interest in chastity and virginity as the means of sacrificing oneself fully to God. Men and women, either alone or in same-sex communities, began to live in strict chastity as an act of devotion to the Lord. Mary became the ideal example, especially for women who took vows of chastity.[5] The church simply expanded Mary's image of virginity to include her entire life as a response to the emerging sentiment in the church as a whole. The belief in the perpetual virginity of Mary is the official teaching of both the Roman Catholic and the Orthodox church. Even John Calvin left the question open.

The most natural way to understand the biblical references, however, is that Mary and Joseph conceived children who were born after Jesus' birth. Matthew makes it clear that Joseph had no sexual relations with Mary, but he limits it to the time "until she gave birth to a son" (Matthew 1:25). The biblical teaching on the virgin conception of Jesus *requires* Mary to be a virgin at the time Jesus was miraculously conceived in her, but nothing in biblical theology requires Mary to be perpetually a virgin. Throughout Scripture God blesses both marriage and the sexual union within marriage. Mary and Joseph were blessed of God with at least six children in addition to Jesus.

Who Are My Mother and Brothers?

Jesus' brothers had grown up in the same home with him, but they couldn't believe what was happening now that Jesus had gone out on his own. He was acting like a pious Jerusalem rabbi! He had a bunch of disciples (such as they were), following him around. Throngs of people were flocking to his hillside meetings. His brothers were asking the same questions their neighbors were asking, "Where did Jesus get this wisdom?" Something had to be done.

These four boys may have grown up around Jesus, but they didn't believe his claims (John 7:5). They even thought it was fun to mock Jesus and sarcastically prod him: "Show yourself to the world" (John 7:2-4). Mary's concern for Jesus and his brothers' embarrassment at what they perceived as Jesus' arrogance brought them to the house where Jesus was preaching. They couldn't get in because of the crowd, or they wouldn't go in because they wanted to talk to Jesus alone. They stood around for a while and finally sent Jesus a message something to the effect of "We would like to talk to you if you can spare some time for your own family."

Jesus got the message. "Your mother and brothers are standing outside," someone said, "wanting to speak to you" (Matthew 12:47). Jesus, however, kept right on talking. Finally, thinking Jesus had not heard, several in the crowd repeated the message, "Your mother and your brothers are outside looking for you" (Mark 3:32).

Jesus, of course, knew their intention. His family had not come to encourage him and assure him of their continued prayer for him. They had come to arrest him, to try to use the club of "good common sense" to turn him from the work the Father had given him to do (Mark 3:21). Mary still had not made the transition in her mind from seeing Jesus as the son of her womb to seeing Jesus as the Servant of the Lord. But everything in Jesus' life had changed. Mary is not calling him from childhood games anymore or ordering him to get more wood for the cooking fire. She can't snap her fingers and turn him away from the path of obedience.

"Who are my mother and my brothers?" Jesus asked. Those who thought they knew the answer to that question soon found that they were wrong. If Jesus had asked me, I would have said, "Jesus, maybe you *are* working too hard! Mary and James and Judas and the other boys are right out there in the courtyard." But Jesus stretched out his arms as if to embrace the crowd of disciples and followers around him and said, "Here are my mother and my brothers! Whoever does God's will is my brother and sister and mother" (Mark 6:34-35).

It's interesting that at this point Jesus did not include Mary among those who were doing the will of God nor (as Luke records it) among those who "hear God's word and put it into practice" (Luke 8:21). The lines are clearly drawn. There is an inner circle of followers and those outside the circle.[6]

Handling Opposition

As far as we know, Jesus never did go out and talk to his family. It seems odd, almost rude, doesn't it? We are a little embarrassed to find Jesus doing something so un-Christlike. On closer inspection, however, we discover that Jesus was demonstrating a very important principle, one that applies to our work in any kingdom enterprise.

Doing the will of God often brings opposition. The critical, fault-finding, "we've-never-done-that-before" Pharisee types are still with us. But sometimes the fiercest opposition to the will of God comes from our own family, from those we love the most, those who have the most emotional power over us. You may know what Jesus was going through from your own personal experience. You may have tried to do what you perceived as the will of God at some point and found the biggest roadblocks put in your way from your own parents or brothers and sisters or your mate. The Pharisees wanted to discredit or discourage Jesus. The opposition from his family was to distract Jesus from the Father's will. When you first hear their reasoning and the concern in their voices, it sounds so compelling, so reasonable. They just want Jesus to lighten up a little. But if he had followed their counsel at this point, it would have turned him from the path the Father had planned for him.

When I pastored a church near a state university, a Jewish college student came to believe in Jesus as Lord through the outreach of one of the campus ministries. In time this young man joined the college group in our church and began to grow in his love for the Lord and for the Word. He would borrow theology books I had labored through in seminary and return them a week later asking for something "a little deeper." Finally he decided to go to seminary himself, and today he is an evangelist.

What those of us who knew him learned much later was that his father had stopped paying his college tuition when the young man trusted Christ. His decision to go to seminary rather than to take his place in the family business was met with disinheritance.

It's difficult as a parent to surrender a child to a ministry that will take that child from us and put him or her in a place of economic struggle or physical danger or continental separation.

Our friends Bill and LaVelle Hamrick found it difficult when their son David sensed God's direction in his life to a work in world missions. Bill and LaVelle had supported missionaries and been involved in mission endeavors for years, but now the sacrifice took on very personal dimensions. It was hard to stand in the airport terminal and say goodby to David and Karen and one-year-old A. J. as they left for South Africa. Bill and LaVelle are thrilled at what God has done through their son and daughter-in-law, but that doesn't take away the pain of separation or the tears that come when they miss their grandson.

Making It Personal

I wonder how willing we are to go to some difficult place to serve God—to make a deliberate decision, for instance, to attend a small, struggling church instead of the exciting megachurch because in the smaller church our gifts can be used more fully. I wonder how willing we are to hold our children, resources, time, commitments with open hands for the Lord to use. We sing "Make Me a Servant" and "Take My Life" on Sunday, but how does that translate into the decisions and priorities of our lives? Are we willing *not* to take the next promotion at work so we can continue to have the time we need to lead a small-group Bible study or be available to parent our children?

Jesus' brothers and mother were willing to use the leverage of common sense and family obligations and even financial security to try to turn Jesus from his obedience to the will of God.

It's purely conjecture, but maybe, as Jesus reflected on this incident, he formulated the stunning teaching we find in Luke 14:26-27: "If anyone comes to me and does not hate his father and mother, his wife and children, his brothers and sisters—yes, even his own life—he cannot be my disciple. And anyone who does not carry his cross and follow me cannot be my disciple." Jesus is obviously overstating the case in order to make his point. In Matthew's account the hyperbole is tamed down a little: "Anyone who loves his father or mother more than me is not worthy of me" (Matthew 10:37).

What Jesus makes very clear is that when there is a conflict between what God dictates and what our families advise or desire, we are to obey God. We find support for that decision within our greater family, the men and women around us who are committed to Christ. Jesus promised that anyone who was forced to give up home or brothers or sisters or father or mother or children because of Christ would find those relationships restored a hundred times within the family of God (Mark 10:29-30).

We aren't told how Mary responded to Jesus' refusal to talk with her that day. I'm sure she continued to be concerned about him. I'm just as certain that she was hurt and maybe even embarrassed by Jesus' behavior toward her. But as Mary reflected on Jesus' words, perhaps she also made one more readjustment in her relationship to this son of hers, one more transition step from parent to follower. Mary had to learn what we need to learn as we grow in spiritual maturity. What Jesus wants us to see is that our choices in life are always to please him first. If we choose parents or children or spouse or any other loyalty over Christ, we are not the fully committed disciple Jesus is seeking. Jesus himself knows how difficult those decisions are. One day he had to make the same choice to ignore a call from his family in order to fully please his Father.

Chapter 12

TO THE CROSS
AND BEYOND

I am writing this chapter on Mary at the cross during the week of Easter. We have just set up for our Good Friday service. No lilies grace the platform. In the center of the worship area a rugged wooden cross looms over the congregation. A purple cloth and a crown of thorns are the only decorations. After the people who helped set up had left, I sat in the auditorium alone for a long time. It's been an emotional few weeks for me, and I don't really know why. At every service, as we've traced the path Jesus walked through his arrest and trial and death, I've been close to tears. Last Sunday I sobbed through a song as the soloist described the dying Savior.

I can only begin to imagine the grief and terror that went through Mary's heart as she stood at the foot of the cross and watched her son suffer. Mary had come to Jerusalem for the Passover just like she did every year. But this time as she approached the city, singing the traditional psalms of ascent with the other pilgrims, Mary sensed that something was dreadfully wrong. If she came to the city on the day of preparation, she may have heard the shouts of the people—not shouts of praise, but angry shouts, murderous shouts. She could make out the words as she came into the court around the temple. The sound came from the Fortress of Antonia, the Roman army barracks next to the temple. All she heard was, "Crucify! Crucify!"

Mary looked in vain for one of the disciples of Jesus. Not one of them was anywhere in sight, until she caught a glimpse of John rushing across the outer court. When she caught up to him, his face was gray. Through panic and sobs, he blurted out the chilling story of Jesus' arrest, the contrived trials and the final verdict. Before she could begin to comprehend what was happening, Mary was holding on to John's arm, stumbling up a rocky hill outside the city. To her horror, her own son was hanging there on a cross.

Woman, Behold Your Son

Execution in Jesus' day was designed to be public and torturously slow. Most of us have never witnessed an execution; the average citizen of Judea had seen dozens.[1] No one paid much attention to criminals as they were marched out to die. They got about as much notice as a funeral procession does today.

Contrary to most of the pictures we see of Jesus bearing his cross, the condemned did not drag the entire cross to the place of execution. The stake, the upright post of the cross, stayed on Calvary's hill. The crossbeam was chained to the arms and carried through the streets for all to see. A sign hung around the neck, stating the person's crime. The same sign would be nailed to the cross so everyone watching the gruesome spectacle would realize that those who dared to rebel against Roman authority paid a supreme price.

Once the execution squad reached the hill of death, the condemned were offered drugged wine to dull the initial pain. The women of Jerusalem provided the drink as a final act of mercy to those about to die. Jesus tasted the wine but refused it. The cup of suffering he was about to drink would be faced in full consciousness.

The condemned were then quickly stripped of clothes and laid down on the cross. Five-inch nails were hammered through the wrists. The cross was then lifted up and dropped in a hole that had held dozens of crosses before. The person's legs were pushed up so the knees bent slightly, and the feet were nailed in place.

Jesus was on the cross six hours. Scripture records that during those hours he spoke seven times. After his prayer for the Father's forgiveness on those who crucified him (Luke 23:34) and his promise of a home in paradise to the repentant thief (Luke 23:43), Jesus turned his eyes to the little band of people standing below him. John was there, the only disciple courageous enough to come close to the cross.[2] He is the one who records this tender scene as Jesus commits Mary into the disciple's care: "When Jesus saw his mother there, and the disciple whom he loved standing nearby, he said to his mother, 'Dear woman, here is your son,' and to the disciple, 'Here is your mother.' From that time on, this disciple took her into his home" (John 19:26-27).

In his dying hours, under such horrifying circumstances that he could be excused from responsibility, Jesus reached out in care for his mother. Even when he was paying the price of humanity's sin, Jesus was thinking of his mother's future. Probably none of Jesus' brothers had come to believe in him yet. So, rather than assume that they would care for Mary as she grew older, Jesus entrusted her care to a faithful disciple.

John tells us that three other women stood with Mary at the cross. One was Mary's sister, not mentioned by name.[3] The second was Mary, the wife of Clopas, who was also the mother of an apostle called James the younger. The third woman was Mary Magdalene, a women whom Jesus had delivered from demonic oppression (Luke 8:2). Four hearts were united in grief.

We discover something interesting when we compare what the other Gospel writers tell us about the group at the cross. In Mark 15:40 Salome is referred to as one of the women in the place of "[Jesus'] mother's sister" mentioned in John 19:25. In Matthew's account this woman is called the mother of Zebedee's sons (Matthew 27:56). If we put the three statements together, we can conclude that the sister of Mary was Salome, the mother of Zebedee's children. Two of Zebedee's sons were among the twelve disciples of Jesus: James (a different James from the son of Clopas) and John the writer of the fourth Gospel. James and John then were Jesus' cousins.

Since John is reluctant to mention his own name in his Gospel, he may have been similarly reluctant to mention his mother's name. He calls himself "the disciple whom Jesus loved" and his mother "[Mary's] sister." John's kinship to Jesus physically and his loyalty to Jesus spiritually may explain why Jesus entrusted his mother to John's care.

In a society that seems increasingly resentful of its older citizens and even of our aging parents, Jesus' example makes us take a long look at our own attitudes and responsibilities. The debate over physician-assisted suicide and euthanasia is already on the national stage, and the volume of the debate will only increase. If any segment of our society should model care and sacrifice for the sick and aging and dependent, it should be those of us who claim to follow Christ.

But I think there is more in this scene than just Jesus' concern for his mother. We are given a glimpse into the depth of the compassion Jesus has for each of us, and the concern he has for our very human needs. You may be grieving as you read these pages. You may find yourself discouraged or lonely or sick. In our despair it's easy to think that no one understands and no one really cares. But this same Jesus has not forgotten you. He cares intensely about every detail of your life.

Simeon's Sword

A flood of memories must have swept over Mary as she watched her son's life drain away. I'm sure she remembered the day in the temple when old Simeon had taken her baby in his arms and proclaimed him to be the Messiah. That old man had whispered some very strange words to Mary as he gave Jesus back to her. He told her that a sword would pierce her soul.

Mary had pondered those words for thirty years, wondering what they meant. Now, standing in the blood-soaked dirt underneath a cross, she knew. Her first-born son, the son of her strength, was dying. No song came from Mary's lips that day. No words of hers are recorded either. She had been the first person to hold the head that now carried a crown of thorns. Like all parents, Mary had examined carefully the tiny hands and feet of her new baby—hands and feet that were now nailed to the cross. Jesus' disciples may desert him, his own people despise him, but his mother stands at his cross.

Mary's grief went beyond her own loss and agony. Nailed to that cross was not only Mary's son but Israel's Deliverer, the One countless believers had longed and prayed for. With his death, the hopes of generations of faithful men and women died too. Even though he spoke words of care to Mary, Jesus offered no explanation for what was happening on the cross. The darkness of Friday was dispelled only by the light of Sunday morning.

We don't know how long Mary stood with John at the scene. John simply says that "from that time, this disciple took her into his home" (John 19:27). Perhaps Mary was there when Jesus breathed his last and when his body was taken from the cross. Mary, cradling the wounded, lifeless body of Jesus, has inspired artists through all the centuries of the church.

We don't know when Mary heard about the empty tomb either. Jesus appeared to several individuals and groups of followers in the days following his resurrection, but nowhere does Scripture say that Jesus appeared to Mary. The apostle Paul tells us that Jesus *did* appear to his brother James shortly after the resurrection (1 Corinthians 15:7).[4] Mary and Jesus' brothers certainly came to believe that Jesus had risen from the dead, because forty days after the resurrection they are gathered in Jerusalem with Jesus' followers (Acts 1:14). We can assume that Mary and Jesus' family were also with the other believers on the Day of Pentecost when the Spirit came upon them in dramatic power (Acts 2). Mary takes her place neither apart from the other Christians nor above them. She is included in the company of those who were followers of her son.

Mary After Pentecost

With the single passing reference to her in Acts, we never again read of Mary in the unfolding story of the early church. At some time after the crucifixion Mary most likely told her story personally to Luke. This would explain how he was able to incorporate such great detail about the conception and birth of Jesus in his Gospel, including Mary's hymn of adoration to the Lord (Luke 1:46-55). We can only speculate as to what happened to Mary from there. One church tradition says that she died at the place where the Church of the Dormition stands outside Jerusalem. Another tradition says that she died in Ephesus in the home and under the care of the apostle John.

Her tomb is said to be located near the tomb of the apostle in Ephesus.[5]

In the developing theology of the church, Mary was not given much place during the first three centuries of doctrinal debate. The early church had to hammer out issues like the Trinity and a proper understanding of the person of Christ. The earliest church fathers seldom mention Mary. When they do speak about her, it is always in connection with Jesus' physical birth and incarnation.[6]

By the fourth century, however, Mary had become more and more elevated in the popular belief of Christians and in the teaching of the church. In the early Apostles' Creed and the Nicene Creed (A.D. 325), we read that Jesus was born of the virgin Mary. It's a simple historical reference. At the Council of Ephesus in A.D. 431 and again at the Council of Chalcedon in A.D. 451, however, Mary's eminence was forged into the doctrinal fabric of the church. While the councils declared Jesus to be both fully human and fully divine, the church leaders also called Mary *theotokos*—not merely the mother of Jesus but the Mother of God.[7] The title was originally intended to say something about Mary's son: that he was God in human flesh. It became, however, a term used to give Mary an exalted place. Both the Roman Catholic Church and the Eastern Orthodox churches trace their official veneration of Mary to the declaration of the Councils of Ephesus and Chalcedon.

By the end of the sixth century, miraculous stories about Mary's death began to make their way into the teaching of the church. Gregory bishop of Tours (in what is today France) was the first church father to promote this in his writings, teaching that Mary was glorified and taken bodily into heaven at the moment of her death.[8] That belief, called the bodily assumption of Mary, was later declared to be the official teaching of the Roman Catholic Church by Pope Pius XII in 1950.

The early medieval church portrayed Mary as the greatest of those whom God loves. She began to be revered as the greatest of the saints and the one to whom even the angels bow in adoration. Theologians as early as the fifth century referred to Mary as the queen of heaven (a figure drawn from the image in Revelation 12:1-2).[9] The same theologians went on to say that when Jesus entrusted Mary to John's care, he was in effect entrusting Mary to all of his followers through the centuries of the church.

One issue that was debated for a long time in the Catholic Church centered around Mary's conception. Was Mary conceived like the rest of humanity with a fallen human nature, or was she protected in some way from sin's contamination? Augustine, the great theologian of the fifth century, proposed that Mary was the "great exception" when it came to the issue of inheriting a sinful human nature. Bernard of Clairvaux, one of the most powerful preachers of the Middle Ages, disagreed. He said that Mary had been redeemed by Christ like every other believer. Mary may have lamented Jesus' death because he was her son, but she also rejoiced because he was her Savior. Thomas Aquinas also taught that Mary was a partaker of original sin like the rest of humanity and the proof was that she suffered one of sin's consequences—she died.

By 1439 theologians at the Council of Basil had come to a consensus that the immaculate conception of Mary was "a pious doctrine," and they declared that any teaching contrary to that belief was forbidden. The Protestant Reformers found this particular doctrine unbiblical and left much of the veneration of Mary behind when they separated from the Roman Church. In 1854 Pope Pius IX made the immaculate conception of Mary an article of faith, a dogma binding on the entire Catholic Church. The Catholic Church teaches that Mary was conceived normally from her parents but was preserved from the stain of sin by a miraculous work of God. Catholic theologians often extend this doctrine to Mary's entire life. She not only was untainted by Adamic sin but lived a life in which she avoided sin completely.[10]

The development of Marian theology in the Catholic Church is far from over. Since 1993 Pope John Paul II has received over four million petitions asking him to exercise the power of papal infallibility to proclaim a new dogma of the faith: that Mary is "Co-Redemptrix, Mediator of All Graces and Advocate for the People of God."[11] Among the supporters of the proposed doctrine were the late Mother Teresa of Calcutta and nearly five hundred bishops and forty-two cardinals in the Catholic Church. If the pope declares such a teaching to be a dogma, Catholics would be obliged to believe that "Mary participates in the redemption achieved by her son, that all graces that flow from the suffering and death of Jesus Christ are granted only through Mary's intercessions with her son, and that all prayers and petitions from the faithful on earth must likewise flow through Mary, who brings them to the attention of Jesus."[12] Mother Angelica, the host of a popular Catholic television program, believes the proposed dogma "would save the world from great catastrophe."

Visions of Virgin Mary

In our local newspaper this week a small article told the story of "miraculous visions of the Virgin Mary on Yakima Valley [Washington] highway signs." Thousands of people were drawn to a sign outside Sunnyside, Washington, creating traffic jams and safety hazards. Some claimed that a rainbow emanated from the sign. People got out of their cars to say prayers, light candles and sing hymns.

Along with the development of official doctrinal teaching within the Catholic and Orthodox churches, there has been a phenomenal resurgence of popular, folk religion centering on Mary. Visions or apparitions of Mary continue to draw throngs of people hoping for a glimpse of Mary or a miraculous healing or some message for their lives. Some of the appearances of Mary have been given official sanction by the Catholic Church. Most claims are neither approved nor denied by church authorities. The bishop of Yakima said he was withholding judgment. The highway department said that what people were seeing on the road signs may have been caused by the oxidation of a chemical coating on the signs.

In the last two thousand years, scholars estimate that more than twenty thousand appearances or apparitions of Mary have been reported. More than four hundred have been reported in the twentieth century alone. The abundance of visions from around the world has prompted some Catholic lay ministers and priests to declare that we are approaching a new "Age of Mary" in the next millennium. The Catholic church has officially recognized only a few of the reported apparitions; most of the reports are not denied but receive no official sanction. The church has put its approval on the appearances of Mary in Fatima, Portugal, in 1917. Three children saw Mary six times over the summer of that year. Probably the most famous modern site of a reported appearance of Mary is Medjugorje in Bosnia-Herzegovina. Six children have seen visions of Mary since 1981. While the Catholic Church has not officially sanctioned those appearances as genuine, ten to twenty million Catholics have visited the area.

Making It Personal

How should we as evangelical Christians respond to the beliefs of the Catholic Church and the reports of the appearances of Mary? I think two bedrock biblical truths will help us sort it out. The first foundational truth to keep in mind is that Jesus

Christ is to be preeminent in everything. We must reject any belief, any vision that takes the focus of our worship and devotion away from Christ as Lord.

The second truth we must cling to is the authority of Scripture. Catholic doctrines about Mary are based largely on church traditions and papal declarations, not biblical teaching. Nowhere in Scripture are we commanded or encouraged to pray to Mary or to any other saint. Worship, devotion, service, veneration are always directed to God alone.

If Mary was to be such a key part of the liturgy and devotion of Christian, why are the Scriptures silent about it? Apart from the historical references in the Gospels and Acts, the New Testament is silent about Mary. In all the letters of Paul instructing the church on doctrine and obedience to God, Mary is referred to only once and never by name. In Galatians 4:4 Paul says that Jesus was "born of a woman, born under law." Furthermore, the Bible never hints or suggests that a believer who has died will ever appear on earth or announce a message from God or intervene to bring about a miracle. *Every* spiritual experience is to be measured against the truth of Scripture.

Mary is a wonderful model of humility and sacrifice and willing obedience to God. But the focus of our love is on Christ alone.

Chapter 13

LIVING
A LEGACY

*T*om Skaff, Steve Aikman and I meet every other week for breakfast. But we don't get together just to share a meal and the latest Dilbert jokes. We meet to hold each other accountable to live godly lives. A few months ago we began talking about our funerals. We challenged each other to think about what we wanted the significant people in our lives to say about us after we die. That exercise may sound pretty morbid, but I wonder if you have ever thought of what your family will remember most about you. What legacy are you leaving behind in the lives of the people you work with or the people you worship with? The longer the three of us thought about it, the more we were motivated to cultivate Christlike qualities in our lives right now.

As we catch our final glimpses of Mary in the New Testament, we begin to sense the impact of her life and example on our lives as Christians. Mary's spiritual legacy challenges me in at least three areas of my walk with Christ—areas that I struggle with often.

First, Mary is a enduring model of willing obedience to God. Unfortunately, we've allowed Mary's gender to cloud the power of her example. Mary too often is pictured as the submissive woman or wife when in fact she submits to God as his servant. Mary did not know what her willingness to obey God's invitation to be the mother of the Messiah would bring into her life. She only knew that the Lord was the most important person. She had a heart that was willing to submit to God even before she was asked.

Most of us think it would be easy to obey God if we had a visit from an angel like Mary did or if we heard God's audible voice. What we haven't grasped is that a willing heart is developed and nurtured as we obey what we already know. Our problem is not in getting *more* direction from God but in obeying what we already understand.

My frustration is that I want God to tell me *where* I should be when God is far more concerned that I become *what* he wants me to be. I want a course laid out in my life with all the blanks filled in. But God is far more focused on the development of my character than on the advancement of my career.

I don't know of any verse in the Bible that will tell you what classes you should take in college next semester. There's no passage that will tell you what job offer to accept or who specifically you should marry. Nothing is said directly in Scripture about *where* I should be as a believer, but *what* God wants me to be is made abundantly clear.

Would you like to know God's will for you today? I obviously don't know you, but I can tell you that part of his will for you is that in everything you give thanks. I know that is God's will because God's Word says so in 1 Thessalonians 5:18. God's will is also that you grow progressively more like Christ and progressively less like the sinful world around you (1 Thessalonians 4:3). God's will according to Ephesians 5:17-18 is that you become filled or controlled by the Holy Spirit. God's will for you at work tomorrow is that you carry out your responsibilities honestly and diligently, as if Jesus were the one you were trying to please (Ephesians 6:5-6).

God's direction in our lives comes to us as we develop godly character, and we develop godly character by obeying what God has already said to us in his Word. I have found that as I become *what* God wants me to be, he has had very little difficulty breaking in on my life and putting me *where* he wants me to be. Mary did not become obedient when Gabriel stood in her presence. Mary, even at a young age, had cultivated a heart of obedience to God. When the moment of decision came, Mary had already disciplined herself to willingly submit to the One who reigned in her life as Lord.

A Matter of Obedience

Karen Karper lives a solitary life of poverty in the hills of West Virginia. She has embraced a life of dependence on God voluntarily. The quiet of her solitude was shattered one day by a call from a friend in desperate need of one hundred dollars. As she listened to the frantic story, Karen realized that one hundred dollars was exactly half the amount in her checking account.

"How soon do you need the money?" she asked. Then she heard another voice, quiet but direct: "Give it to him." With a step of faith, she promised to send the money. She wrote out the check and climbed the hill to her mailbox beside the road. The mail from the day before was there, and she glanced through it without much interest. Back at the house, she sat on the porch to open the letters. A check fell out of one of the envelopes—a check for one hundred dollars. She thanked God immediately. "Your timing, Lord, is utterly fantastic." As she thought about this unexpected provision, Karen concluded, "Once again I had experienced how my Faithful God provided for my every need, even forestalling a single day of worry."[1] The careful and difficult cultivation of an obedient life blossomed into the fragrant flower of a spirit willing to do whatever God desired.

Karen Karper's obedience, like Mary's, was not forced or extracted under pressure. We have a desire to serve those we genuinely love. You may find yourself responsible to care for an aging parent or a sick friend. As difficult as those situations can be at times, sacrificial love has to lie at the heart of that care. Otherwise we sink quickly into resentful complaint. In our marriages we learn to anticipate the other person's needs and desires. Wherever our mate wants to eat out or whatever our mate wants to watch on television is fine with us. The same willingness ought to mark our walk with the Lord. A tender spirit toward God doesn't have to be pushed or threatened into obedience. A suggestion, the slightest nudge from the Spirit, is enough to send us joyfully on our way to do whatever will please the One we love most. I wish my own life approached Mary's level of humble, joyful, extravagant obedience.

Meditating on God's Goodness

Another root of Mary's legacy that I want to take hold in the soil of my life is her willingness to quietly reflect on God's character and on God's activity for good in the circumstances in which she found herself. Quiet thought and biblical meditation are almost lost disciplines in our hectic world. We want fast food, instant solutions to our problems and effortless spiritual maturity. Most of the books and seminars on prayer focus on what we do in prayer and what we say. Very few resources discuss the place of silence in prayer or the importance of listening in prayer for God's insight and instruction. Our time in God's Word is just one more demand on our overcrowded "to do" list. When we've finished, we rush on through our day and barely give a moment of thought to what we've read or how it might affect our priorities or responsibilities.

Mary had learned the value of quiet reflection. In her song of praise to God, she reflects out loud on the marvelous character and wonderful works of God. Her song emerges from her own meditation on who God is and how he is working in her life and in the life of the believing community around her. When Jesus is born, Mary treasures and stores away the events surrounding the birth. Later, in her own thoughts, she examines those events one after another. When Jesus as a young boy stays behind in Jerusalem, frightening his parents, Mary questions him but then reflects on the significance of all that had happened. In the insightful words of one student of Mary's legacy: "Mary does not wait passively for someone else to explain things to her; she takes an active part by thinking, reflecting, considering matters."[2]

Don't trivialize Mary's quiet pondering, as if she is doing nothing more than gluing pictures in a family scrapbook. Mary is demonstrating the value of the difficult spiritual work of reflection, quiet meditation focused on God's character and on his purposes in our lives.

Fortunately there are some resources designed to help us sharpen this particular aspect of our spiritual walk. A search of your local Christian bookstore will lead you to some excellent resources written to provide the structure for regular, systematic reading and personal Bible study. Look also for material that provides suggestions for personal reflection and prayer.[3] Reading the meditative writings of Christian sisters and brothers of the past makes us pause and think carefully about the call of Christ in our lives. You can't skim through Augustine or

Teresa of Ávila. Their profound words and quiet contemplation on the ways of God slow our minds and steady our hearts so we can ponder the wonders of God's love and grace.

The Line of the Unknown

The aspect of Mary's spiritual example that has made the deepest impression on me is her vulnerability to all that God wanted to do in her life. The word *vulnerability* does not mean that Mary was a weak, helpless victim. It is a courageous word. Most of us don't step forward to embrace change or struggle. We aren't risk-takers, especially in our walk with the Lord. But Mary was willing to step across the line of the unknown. She wasn't foolishly rushing in where angels fear to tread. She was simply willing to open herself fully to everything that came from God's hand. She was willing to walk with the Lord through joy and through pain because she had learned to trust the Shepherd of her life. She had learned that the place of safety was near to God even in the most desperate circumstances.

Mary was willing to respond positively to God's call to bear the Messiah even if it meant losing everyone she held dear, including Joseph. She was willing to stand at the cross and watch up close as her son died. She accepted the incredible pain of the sword in her heart because she knew God had led her to the foot of that cross.

We are very willing to accept what we perceive as good and pleasant from God, but we aren't very willing to embrace the plan of God if it leads to suffering or loss. We love to stand in a gathering of Christians and tell about the remarkable evidences of God's power in our lives. We don't hear many testimonies, however, about the fellowship of Christ's suffering. Bearing in our bodies the dying of Jesus just doesn't hold much appeal in the church of the prosperous and in the land of plenty.

Mary stepped up to embrace whatever glory and whatever pain the will of God brought to her. She endured the difficulties not just for the eternal glory that stretched ahead of her as a redeemed child of God. She was vulnerable to both tragedy and celebration simply for the joy of serving her God.

Following in Mary's Steps

Many serious Catholics will admit that some Catholics have elevated Mary almost to the level of deity. That excessive devotion needs to be corrected. Many serious evangelicals will admit that most evangelicals have ignored Mary as a biblical model of servanthood and godly obedience. That shameful neglect needs to be corrected too. Every Christian will confess that worship and glory and adoration belong to God alone. Some day we will all stand redeemed before the Father, and we will find ourselves conformed perfectly not to the image of Mary but to the image of Mary's son, Jesus Christ. Until that day, we are to run the race of this life with endurance and faith. Mary is one of the great company of witnesses urging us on and modeling the kind of life we are to live. We can certainly find encouragement in the race from Mary's life, but our eyes are fixed on Jesus, our Redeemer, the One who washed us from our sins and who loves us with an eternal love.

This December when you put out the nativity set for Christmas, give thanks to God for Mary's courageous example. Strive to display the same willing obedience in your life that Mary models. But then give praise and worship to Mary's son, Jesus Christ, who displayed the most sacrificial obedience of all when he stepped from heaven's glory to become our Savior.

"Whatever *he* says, do it!"

Notes

Chapter 2: Listening to an Angel

[1]Origen, the church father, puts this claim in the mouth of a man named Celsus (*Contra Celsum* 1.32), quoted in Robert Stein, *Jesus the Messiah: A Survey of the Life of Christ* (Downers Grove, Ill.: InterVarsity Press, 1996), p. 33.

[2]The Roman Catholic prayer based on this passage says, "Hail, Mary, full of grace." The translation "full of grace" is drawn from the Latin Vulgate, which reads *gratia plena*. The phrase "highly favored" is a more accurate translation of the Greek text of Luke's Gospel. Stephen Benko, *Protestants, Catholics and Mary* (Valley Forge, Penn.: Judson, 1968), p. 19. The full text of the Ave Maria or Hail Mary prayer reads: "Hail, Mary, full of grace; / the Lord is with thee. / Blessed art thou among women, / and blessed is the fruit of thy womb, Jesus. / Holy Mary, Mother of God, / pray for us sinners, / now and at the hour of our death. Amen." Forms of this prayer date from the eleventh century in the Western church and from as early as the sixth century in the Eastern church. The form of the prayer said today was not popular until the sixteenth century. Most Catholics are familiar with the Hail Mary from its use in praying the Rosary (*The Encyclopedia of Catholicism* [San Francisco: HarperSanFrancisco, 1995], p. 602).

[3]Traditionally, Elizabeth has been referred to as Mary's cousin, but Luke describes their relationship with a very general word meaning any female relative.

Chapter 3: Amazed in God's Presence

[1]Tradition places the home of Zechariah and Elizabeth at Ain Kerem, a village in Judea, five miles west of Jerusalem, about eighty miles from Nazareth. Darrell Bock, *Luke*, Baker Exegetical Commentary on the New Testament (Grand Rapids, Mich.: Baker Book House, 1994), 1:140.

[2]The term *theotokos* is more accurately translated "God-bearer." It is a combination of the Greek words *theos* ("God") and *tokos* (from the verb *tiktein*, "to bear, give birth to").

Chapter 5: Dusting Off the Nativity Set

[1]See Paul Maier, *In the Fullness of Time* (San Francisco: HarperSanFrancisco, 1991), pp. 6-7.

[2]Many more details about the Church of the Nativity and modern-day Bethlehem can be found in ibid., pp. 34-42.

Chapter 6: Holding God in Our Arms

[1]See, for example, Numbers 24:2; Judges 6:34; 14:6; 1 Samuel 10:10; 2 Chronicles 24:20; Ezekiel 11:5.

Chapter 8: Finding the Path

[1]A collection of these apocryphal stories can be found in J. K. Elliott, ed., *The Apocryphal Jesus* (New York: Oxford University Press, 1996). This story is on pp. 28-29.

[2]Ibid., p. 25.

[3]Ibid., p. 26.

[4]One way to cultivate a deeper appreciation for the faith and the freedoms we enjoy is to read the stories of those who have died for their loyalty to Christ. James and Marti Hefley have written a powerful book about Christian martyrs in the twentieth century called *By Their Blood* (Grand Rapids, Mich.: Baker Book House, 1996). In her book *In the Lion's Den* Nina Shea writes about areas of the world where Christians are persecuted today (Nashville: Broadman and Holman, 1997). Another resource focused more on individual martyrs is Susan Bergman, ed., *Martyrs* (San Francisco: HarperCollins, 1996).

[5]Josephus (*Antiquities of the Jews* 17.6.4; 17.9.3) placed the death of Herod shortly after an eclipse of the moon and before a Passover celebration in Jerusalem. In 4 B.C. there was a lunar eclipse on the night of March 12/13, one month before Passover. There are other possible years in which the same events coincide, but the best evidence favors March/April, 4 B.C., as the date of Herod's death. The date of 6-5 B.C. for Jesus' birth also fits with Luke's statement (Luke 3:23) that Jesus was "about thirty years of age" in the fifteenth year of the reign of Tiberius Caesar (Luke 3:1), which was A.D. 27/28.

A mistake in calculation resulted in Jesus' being born "before Christ." In A.D. 533 Dionysius Exiguus (Denis the Short) proposed changing the calendar to mark years from the birth of Christ (A.D. or Anno Domini, "in the year of our Lord") rather than from the founding of the city of Rome (A.U.C. or Anno Urbis Conditae, "in the year from the foundation of the city"). He chose 754 A.U.C. as A.D. 1. Modern chronologists can more accurately place Herod's death at 750 A.U.C. or 4 B.C. See Raymond Brown, *The Birth of the Messiah* (New York: Doubleday, 1993), pp. 166-67, and Maier, *In the Fullness of Time*, pp. 24-25 and notes 1 and 2, p. 340.

Chapter 9: Raising God's Son

[1]These accounts can be found in Elliot, *Apocryphal Jesus*, pp. 20-23. Elliot dates the writing of the *Infancy Gospel of Thomas* in the second or third century.

Chapter 10: A Life in the Shadows

[1]Some scholars have used the statement of some Jews in John 6:42 to argue that Joseph was alive during Jesus' ministry: "Is this not Jesus, the son of Joseph, whose father and mother we know? How can he now say, 'I came down from heaven'?" The statement of the crowd, however, simply shows their acquaintance with Joseph. It says nothing about whether he was alive or dead at the time.

The apocryphal book *The History of Joseph the Carpenter* (fourth century A.D.) claims that Joseph was forty years old when he married Mary, was married to her forty-nine years and survived her by one year!

[2]In the papal encyclical *Redemptoris mater*, issued in 1987, Pope John Paul II points

to this passage as evidence for Mary's role as *mediatrix*, one who intercedes with her son for the needs of others. Most Catholic Mariology makes this leap from biblical narrative to a broad theological precept. The passage in John's Gospel, however, points to Jesus' glory, not Mary's.

[3]For a discussion of the purpose of biblical miracles, see my book *Miracles: What the Bible Says* (Downers Grove, Ill.: InterVarsity Press, 1997).

[4]Some Catholic theologians (beginning with Thomas Aquinas) propose a third level of devotion, a hyperveneration above saints but below God, reserved for Mary alone (Victor Buksbazen, *Miriam, the Virgin of Nazareth* [Philadelphia: Spearhead, 1963], pp. 210-11).

[5]Margaret Bunson, comp., *John Paul's Book of Mary* (Huntington, Ind.: Our Sunday Visitor, 1996), p. 17. John Paul II is a devotee of Our Lady of Czestochowa, the patroness of his native Poland. His motto is "I am wholly yours, Mary" *(totus tuus sum, Maria)*, and he has added an *M* to his papal coat of arms in honor of Mary.

Chapter 11: When Answers Don't Come

[1]Mark 3:31-35; 6:3; John 2:12; 7:3-5, 10; Acts 1:14; 1 Corinthians 9:5; Galatians 1:19.

[2]The apocryphal *History of Joseph the Carpenter* (written about A.D. 400) gives the names of Joseph's sons as Judas, Justus, James and Simon, and his daughters as Assia and Lydia (Benko, *Protestants, Catholics and Mary*, p. 114).

[3]Stein, *Jesus the Messiah*, pp. 82-84.

[4]Actually the doctrine of the perpetual virginity of Mary states: (1) Mary was a virgin *before* the conception of Jesus, and his conception occurred without a sexual encounter with a man. (2) Mary remained a virgin *during* the birth of Jesus. In the process of giving birth, the hymen of Mary remained unperforated and intact. (3) Mary had no sexual relationship *after* the birth of Jesus and, of course, bore no other children. This doctrine was declared to be the official teaching of the Catholic Church at the Lateran Council in A.D. 649 under Pope Martin I. It was reaffirmed at the Council of Trent in 1555.

The first part of the doctrine is supported entirely by Scripture. The argument for the second part comes entirely from what Catholic theologians view as the teaching authority of the Catholic Church. Support for the third element of the doctrine comes from church tradition and the view of some church fathers that Jesus' brothers and sisters were not children of Mary.

[5]Raymond Brown, a noted Roman Catholic theologian, has pointed out that Mary chose marriage over celibacy. In his view Mary's virginity is stressed as evidence that Jesus had no earthly father, not as an ideal for Christians to embrace. R. E. Brown, *The Virginal Conception and Bodily Resurrection of Jesus* (New York: Paulist, 1973), pp. 38-40.

[6]On another occasion a woman in the crowd around Jesus shouted, "Blessed is the mother who gave you birth and nursed you." Jesus' reply again seems to leave Mary out: "Blessed rather are those who hear the word of God and obey it" (Luke 11:27-28). When Luke lists the women who followed Jesus during his ministry, several are mentioned by name but not Mary. Even though Luke includes "many

other" women, we would expect Mary to be listed if she had been part of those considered Jesus' disciples (Luke 8:2-3).

Chapter 12: To the Cross and Beyond

[1]"Jews were all too familiar with crucifixion, for even Jewish leaders used it. In the first century B.C. the high priest Alexander Jannaeus crucified eight hundred Pharisees who had revolted against him. In 4 B.C. the Syrian governor crucified two thousand Jews. During the Jewish revolt in A.D. 66-70 Josephus refers to Titus' crucifying five hundred Jews a day! . . . Crucifixion remained the primary form of capital punishment in the Roman Empire until A.D. 337, when Constantine banned it" (Stein, *Jesus the Messiah,* pp. 244-45).

[2]It is possible that Peter witnessed Jesus' death, but from a distance. In 1 Peter 5:1 he calls himself "a witness of Christ's sufferings."

[3]Some translators and scholars find only two other women in this passage: (1) Mary's sister, also named Mary and the wife of Clopas, and (2) Mary Magdalene. This view brings two women into the same family as sisters, both of whom are named Mary! The preferable view is to see a total of four women in this scene: (1) Mary, Jesus' mother, (2) her sister (unnamed), (3) Mary, wife of Clopas, and (4) Mary Magdalene.

[4]Since Paul lists James separately from "all the apostles," most scholars conclude that this is not a reference to James the son of Zebedee or to James the Younger, both members of the original group of twelve apostles, but a reference to the half-brother of Jesus named James (Mark 6:3). This James became a leader in the early church (Acts 15:13; 21:18; Galatians 1:19) and is considered by most evangelical scholars as the author of the New Testament letter of James. Another brother of Jesus, Judas, is probably the author of the small New Testament book of Jude.

[5]These traditions are discussed in Marina Warner, *Alone of All Her Sex: The Myth and Cult of the Virgin Mary* (New York: Vintage, 1983), pp. 86-90.

[6]See the survey of early references to Mary in Raymond Brown et al., eds., *Mary in the New Testament* (New York: Paulist, 1978), pp. 253-57.

[7]Nestorius, the bishop of Constantinople, wanted to refer to Mary as *Christotokos,* the mother of Christ. His opponent Cyril, bishop of Alexandria, insisted on the term *theotokos,* the mother of God.

Evangelical Christians (following Martin Luther and John Calvin) would agree that Mary's child was fully human and fully God, and in that sense Mary is the mother of God. Roman Catholic Mariology goes beyond that point, however, and says that this belief is merely the starting point for a whole doctrine of Mary's divine motherhood. Another idea drawn from the concept of *theotokos* by Catholic theologians is that Mary is the mother of all Christians or the mother of the church since, in a spiritual sense, she gave birth to the body of Christ. For a complete discussion of this dogma and its implications, see Benko, *Protestants, Catholics and Mary,* pp. 26-30.

[8]Ibid., p. 41.

[9]The traditional Roman Catholic interpretation of the woman "clothed with the sun" in Revelation 12 is that she represents Mary, who gave birth to Jesus ("a male child"). Evangelicals (and an increasing number of Catholic interpreters) have identified the woman in John's vision as either the nation of Israel or the believing community. For a survey of the various views, see Alan Johnson, "Revelation," in *The Expositor's Bible*

Commentary (Grand Rapids, Mich.: Zondervan, 1981), 12:512-14.

[10]For a sympathetic but thorough study of the development of doctrines surrounding Mary, see Jaroslav Pelikan, *Mary Through the Centuries* (New Haven, Conn.: Yale University Press, 1996).

[11]Kenneth Woodward has written an excellent article on the contemporary controversy over Mary's place in Catholic belief: "The Meaning of Mary: A Struggle over Her Role Grows Within the Church," *Newsweek,* August 25, 1997, pp. 49-55.

[12]This is Woodward's explanation of the teaching in ibid., p. 49.

Chapter 13: Living a Legacy

[1]Karen Karper's perceptive and challenging story is told in *Where God Begins to Be: A Woman's Journey into Solitude* (Grand Rapids, Mich.: Eerdmans, 1994). The account of the check in the mail comes from pp. 90-91.

[2]Beverly Roberts Gaventa, *Mary: Glimpses of the Mother of Jesus* (Columbia: University of South Carolina Press, 1995), p. 130. I am indebted to Gaventa for her insights into this particular facet of Mary's character.

[3]*The NIV Quiet Time Bible* (Downers Grove, Ill.: InterVarsity Press, 1996) is a wonderful resource that links serious Bible study with reflection and personal application. InterVarsity's LifeGuide Bible Study series takes a similar approach in a more expanded format.

Subject Index

Scripture Index